A.T.T.E.N.D.

A.T.T.E.N.D.

A HUSTLER'S GUIDE TO HACKING COLLEGE

ADRIAN ABRAMS

NEW DEGREE PRESS

A.T.T.E.N.D.

A Hustler's Guide To Hacking College

ISBN   978-1-5445-0002-7 *Paperback*

978-1-5445-0003-4 *Ebook*

CONTENTS

ABOUT THE AUTHOR

Adrian Abrams is a frequent speaker, coach, and trainer to high school students through ATTEND Ventures, a company that provides coaching, training, and advice for students seeking to elevate their academic performance. As an early advocate of mentorship, Adrian routinely helped younger students unlock their academic potential through developing his own methodologies of academic counseling. These experiences led to him developing a true passion for academic counseling and largely inspired this book!

Adrian developed the A.T.T.E.N.D. method while earning Dean's List honors every semester at Georgetown University and seeks to impart said wisdom onto you!

FOREWORD

———

Before moving any further, I would like to give special recognition those that have been absolutely transformative in my life.

- **To God be the glory.** Although I'm still on my own spiritual journey, I would like to thank You for bringing my mother and I from a mighty long way.
- **Rosalind Abrams:** We've been through it all but we're not done yet. Thank you for being a visionary and always instilling within me the drive to achieve greater. Although you may not have grown up with the love and affection you wanted, you ensured I received the love and affection I needed. Lastly, we've done a lot of great things with minimal support from our "family." I think this quote aptly sums up our time together: "Believed in ourselves when nobody else believed us." - Jadakiss
- **Dana Whittaker:** You are a special kind of guidance counselor.

Much like my mother, you had a vision for something greater for me. You and your team provided a lot of great advice along the way, especially during my senior year, and for that I'm eternally grateful.

- **Eric Koester:** In my Instagram bio, I have "The Year of the Visionary" at the bottom. Professor Koester aptly epitomizes what it means to be a visionary and to continue to push the envelope for what is considered to be the norm. I am truly honored to be a part of his pilot class for "The School Book Method."

- **Friends in High School:** Admittedly so, me being absent my senior year has made a huge impact as far as why we're not as close as we were today. Although I'm unsure we'll ever reach that point again considering we are growing into very different people, I am thankful for all the memories we do have whether that was paying for me to eat at Los Burritos, giving me a cell phone when mine broke, or even always letting me come over and eat with your family. Those are memories I wouldn't trade for anything as I truly felt as though you all were my family.

- **Friends in College:** I've said it before and I'll say it again: I owe a majority of my college success to you all. Man, you all have challenged me to think beyond my initial intellectual capacity, been there for some of my greatest triumphs and heartbreaks, avoided unnecessary drama, and have showed me what a loving family is supposed to look like. Thank you all for simply being there and I'm excited to see where all of our paths take us.

- **Anyone Who Has Given Me A Helping Hand:** Although I can't name everyone that has ever helped me in my life, I would like to take this time to recognize you. Because I understand everything being predicated on prior experiences, I feel as though the individual that baby sat me when I was 3 deserves as much thanks as the teacher that rounded my 88 up to a 90 when I was 17. So many people have impacted and all I hope is that I can pay it forward for the next generation of dreamers.

- **To Those That Wanted/Still Want to See My Mother and I Lose:** You can't stop what's already been ordained!

FROM THE AUTHOR:

Coming into Georgetown, one of the biggest things that I realized, early on, was the academic deficit between some of the various diverse student groups here on campus. Diversity can be seen by the various socio-economic classes, region that students grew up in, race, gender, and so on and so forth.

One of the biggest by-products of having such a diverse student population is noticing the degrees of separation between the "haves" and "have nots."

A tangible example would be the deficit between the students that went to top boarding schools, such as Exeter Academy, vs my high school education at a public school, by the name of Willowbrook, in the western suburbs of Chicago and seeing how I'm miles behind them even though, theoretically, we are on the same playing field.

However, as the saying goes, everything is relative.

While initially frustrated by my high school's inability to provide me with resources that other top schools had, I began to grow a deeper appreciation for Willowbrook after comparing it to some of the schools that students less fortunate than me attended. For example, some of my peers went to public schools within failing school districts.

When we would talk about our different academic past experiences and whatnot, their lack of exposure to some of the academic knowledge that I was exposed to in high school was clearly apparent. Pragmatically, this meant that sometimes they didn't recognize they needed a "works cited" page on most college level papers, knowing the standard format for different assignments, being able to take calculus in high school, and so on and so forth.

As a result, I saw that there was a very large degree of separation that ultimately sparked my initial interest in public education and got me curious about the specific point that inequality and inequity are created/occur.

In my opinion, private school is important and it has definitely done its job, as far as preparing our next generation of leaders. But at the same time, I'm coming from the frame of thought that wants everyone to have access to the same opportunities, regardless of socio-economic class, which leads to my passion about public education. In fact, this passion has definitely shaped my collegiate extracurricular involvements as well.

Throughout my time at Georgetown, I have been involved in numerous student groups that are focused on education. Namely, I've worked with the After School Kids Program, which works with that adjudicated or formally adjudicated/ court involved youth in DC. Some of the key aspects of the ASK Program include:

- utilizing a near-peer model, which pairs Georgetown University undergraduate students as tutors and mentors for our youth;
- providing exposure to the college experience, as programming is regularly offered on-campus;
- promoting lifelong-learning and the links among education, earning potential, and self-sufficiency, as well as the skills and behaviors needed to achieve such success; and
- supporting social-justice education and our youth's critical analysis of how they can contribute to a more just world. [Cited from this website: https://csj.georgetown.edu/ask]

In the summer of 2016, I accepted an internship offer with the DC Public School System as a UELIP intern. In this role, I worked on the daily operations that were involved with the creation of DC's first all-male public school, Ron Brown College Preparatory High School. I was tasked with forming the curriculum template, applications, and recruitment vehicles for the school's first mentorship program.

On a technical level, I learned the importance of researching and being open to pivots when creating an entirely new program. On a more personal level, within my short time at DCPS, I had the opportunity to get a rare glimpse into some of the methodological processes an educational system must go through in order to create an entirely new school. In addition, having the opportunity to interact with the staff members of RBCPHS was eye-opening because not only did I get to see what type of individuals were spearheading this groundbreaking initiative, but I also gained invaluable insight from each and every one of them.

Now, I work with the Institute for College Preparation. In my role, I help out facilitating teacher-led discussions and classes during our Saturday Academy's that are entirely focused on getting our students into college and helping prepare them academically to not only matriculate into college but also to continue to attribute to the retention rate in college.

In essence, we want to make sure that they not only survive, but thrive in college.

All in all, all 3 of these experiences have been very pivotal for me, as far as nurturing my educational passion. I didn't even know I had this interest until I matriculated to Georgetown and had the opportunity to start reflecting on my different experiences within all these different spaces and seeing the large degrees of privilege and oppression in that sense.

And so with coming to write this book, I was actually at Google in the summer of 2016 for a week-long externship, entitled the BOLD Immersion Program, and myself, along with several other students, were participating in something called "Design Thinking Workshop". The Design Thinking Workshop was designed to give us insight as to what Google's approach to problem-solving was. Essentially, they took us through their whole workshop and one of the biggest elements of this was called "10X thinking."

10X thinking, in my opinion, is pretty much saying that while you can address one problem, don't just stop there; think of everything unilaterally that can also be solved by looking at this one problem as the core for a centerpiece while still expanding out from there. This frame of thought really stuck with me, to say the least.

To my surprise, we had an opportunity to put this concept into action by actually participating in a practice workshop with the help of several Google facilitators.

So when we put this into practice, I got a chance to talk to my peers about some of the different problems that they might face. Through this workshop, I created the startup idea that this book is based on and it ultimately ended up being an idea that is focused on the intersections of education, business, and technology in a sense of wanting to help students accelerate their academic learning process. Although I did not have the opportunity to develop the idea fully at the end of the summer of 2016, I kept my idea and 10X thinking close to me as I embarked on the fall semester of my junior year in college.

As I enrolled in my coursework for the fall, I ended up taking a class with Professor Eric Koester entitled "Launching The Venture" as a requirement for my Certificate in Entrepreneurship. On the first day of class, he talked about his creativity in wanting to bring innovation to the classroom and teaching students in a new way.

He knew the chances of us actually launching a startup during or after the completion of this course were severely low. Therefore, he wanted to give us something that we could actually take away from the course that would be immensely beneficial for us moving forward whether professionally, socially, whatever. His grand vision for this "something" that could help us achieve the aforementioned was simple: he was going to facilitate the processes of getting our entire class to write a book.

A book? We all smirked and jeered, admittedly so, knowing that he could not be serious.

But he was serious... And here I am!

Crazy? Of course. Audacious? You better believe it. Pretty freaking cool?

You're damn right.

His grand vision for class was for us to write a book that was related to a startup idea that we had. The rationale behind this was for us to be established as an expert in the field related to our startup idea by creating a book full of research and what not. Here was the kicker: he said that if we could put out at least a B+ manuscript at the end of the semester, we would have the opportunity to become fully published authors. This opportunity would only be offered to our class, and none thereafter, as we were the pilot class. He also detailed about the endless possibilities stemming from becoming a published author including speaking engagements, credibility, etc.

The crazy thing is I was originally supposed to study abroad this semester but ultimately pushed it back to the spring.

Timing is everything.

I could not help but think that my prior collegiate experiences and summer ventures helped propel me to be in a position to turn some of my dreams into reality simply by enrolling, and doing well, in this course.

I also could not help but think:

LET'S GET IT!

* * *

When I was going through book development, I was thinking about ways to relate this startup idea to an entire book topic. As I was thinking pragmatically and fundamentally about what my startup idea was trying to achieve, I realized I wanted to give students access and insight as to what's going to help them academically in college.

Then I thought to myself, "Okay, how do I make myself an expert in this field. Okay, I've gotten pretty good grades and have had many great opportunities but do not really feel as though I am the exception; in fact, my results can be replicated... But how do I really transcribe that information into something that's easily digestible for a potential audience?"

Then I remembered that I also read a book this summer called "How to Win Friends and Influence People" and how just a simple how-to book sort of changed my whole paradigm as far as my perception of how-to books because, prior to reading that one, I didn't really like them. After reading that book, however, I was like "wow I actually learned a lot from it."

Therefore, that framework inspired me to create *A.T.T.E.N.D.: A Hustler's Guide To Hacking College* with the goal of painting me as an expert in the field of academic learning, academic excellence, and talking about the different ways you can ascend into the ranks of academic excellency.

I also wanted to help students understand that whether you have peers in college from elite school systems, students from schools like mine, or students from systematically disadvantaged schools, there are still recurring themes between the top performing students that can be implemented and replicated into one's own repertoire despite your background or self-perceived academic inabilities (that are most likely rooted in fallacy).

* * *

As I started developing the book, many of the questions I got early on were concerned with my plan to tailor my book to my audience (college students) even though there are, ideally, so many different high school students from so many different backgrounds. Would it be possible to both generalize and tailor it, or would I have to settle for either/or?

The biggest way that I am trying to tailor it would be through the use of personal narratives. Although most of the students that I've interviewed are from Georgetown, they come from a variety of different backgrounds due to the diverse student populations Georgetown pulls from. Some come from the elite backgrounds, some are coming from the middle class background, and some are coming from low-income backgrounds.

I'm hoping that the use of personal narratives from different backgrounds will allow any reader to see themselves, at least in some regard, throughout my use of the different narratives.

At the same time, I have to acknowledge that there are a lot of general things that some of the most successful students are doing, quite frankly, and in order to replicate their level of academic success, I would argue that you sort of have to get on board with that.

Therefore, the general trends that are performed by students were laid out as the outline for success. However, to ensure that tailoring is still evident, I incorporated different variations of the set principles. In order to truly illustrate this point, I will provide an example.

Let's say that you and I are in the same class and just received the syllabus. One of the first assignments that is required is due in two weeks and we both agree that we need to get the assignment done in advance. This is an example of us finding commonality in understanding the general rule of doing our work well in advance. However, the next step incorporates tailoring the general rule as you see fit.

After discussing what needs to be done, we have different methodological preferences:

A) you might say that you want to finish the assignment four days in advance

B) I might say that I want to finish the assignment a day and a half in advance.

Although we both have a different pragmatic approach to this rule, we are still exuberating the same general trend.

I also want you, the reader, to connect with me on a deeper level in order to allow these lessons to truly resonate with you. Therefore, I want to talk a little bit about myself and my background in order to establish a sense of familiarity. I want to take you through some of my experiences as a low-income student, having had (and still having) bouts with poverty, being homeless, being a working class student, and different comparable things that have shaped me into the person I am today.

In spite of all those inhibiting factors, I still have had amazing opportunities. Without a doubt, a lot of these opportunities were made possible by being in the top of my class because I hacked college.

* * *

Although there are a variety of different reasons for why you might be here reading this book, if you are seeking academic excellence, I want you to know that I've got your back. Even if you don't come from a background comparable to mine, I've still got your back.

However, please understand that the purpose of this book is not to be a feel-good story. The purpose of me divulging so much about my life is not to create "trauma-porn" that showcases how grit, resiliency, and determination allowed me to pull myself up by the bootstraps and overcome all the odds.

Rather, the purpose is to allow you to have the full framework to help you understand the contexts and derivations on how I came up with the realizations about what it takes to be successful in college.

Now, I want to impart the same lessons that have been so fruitful on my life to you, the reader.

Lastly, I want to unpack a very important fallacy in this book:

You will need to sacrifice sleep in order to do well academically.

Nope. Take it from a guy who sleeps soundly every night including finals week.

I simply refuse to believe sacrificing sleep is the way to go (and turns out most sleep research shows this is correct — being sleep deprived is equivalent to being moderately buzzed, which seems like a stupid way to take an exam if you ask me.) I am very much the type of person to want to get 7-8 hours of sleep a night and still take a 1-hour nap in a given day.

Whenever I tell my peers this, they are always initially shocked and assume that I don't do anything. However, if we actually check my resume for my extracurricular activities, view my social experiences on Instagram or Snapchat and check the stats on grades and the courses I am taking, it is plain to see that this notion could not be deviating further from the truth.

Remember, college is a process that can be hacked. You just have to know the rules and then be smart about your approach. Do that and you really can have it all.

Thank you all for your first steps in embarking on this journey with me.

Enjoy!

PROLOGUE

"I know you are thinking about taking her, but don't."

"My dad is renting us a limo to get to the dance. You should come to the dance with me. *smiley-face*"

"Don't make me beg, but I'm begging."

My cell phone was blowing up. It was less than a week until the Homecoming dance and I had options. It felt good to have options. Well, it was also bad because that meant I had to tell two people no — at least. Nevertheless, options were good.

It was homecoming week during my senior year of high school. The leaves were falling, pumpkin spice lattes were making their resurgence, and life was good.

While in the suburbs of Chicago, I attended a good—not great public high school. For everything that my school might have lacked, however, it made up for in other ways. For example, every time we walked through the hallways, encouragement and love were evident at every corner. In addition, my high school attained success in sending students to their desired trajectory whether it was trade school, the work force, or four-year university; it offered something for everyone.

Me? I was on the latter path.

I was working diligently with my guidance counselors on my college applications, researching many scholarships that I was a seemingly qualified candidate for, captain of the best football team we had in years, and, to top it all off, had 3 girls hoping I'd ask them to the homecoming dance! Rumor was, I'd probably be in the running for homecoming king.

Yeah, I was on top of the world!

My guidance counselors tried to give me the full scoop on the college application process. I needed to develop a list of "safety" schools (schools that I was virtually guaranteed to get into), "match" schools (acceptance wasn't a given but I matched very well with what they were looking for), and "reach" schools (schools that may be a long shot). Admittedly so, my counselors and I were more concerned with reach schools; especially the Ivy League.

The Ivy League schools are considered reaches for almost anyone. Furthermore, once you consider applying to schools that are in the "elite" category, you are essentially applying through a crapshoot. I know multiple stories of kids getting into Harvard and Yale but rejected by the University of Pennsylvania or Duke University. Due to all of the variability, nothing is ever a given.

Despite the odds not being in my favor, I felt as though that was where I belonged. My mother told me from a very early age that I was *destined* to attend either Harvard, Yale, or Princeton, referred to as "The Holy Grail" in some circles. Because I was told this as a child, I ensured my actions were purposeful so that my *destiny* would be fulfilled.

Although my test scores were low (26 on the ACT), my GPA (4.5/4.0) and extracurricular involvement was high and I received backing from my guidance counselors. I was on track to be one of the few students to come out of my high school to make it to an Ivy League school and we all had the genuine belief I was going to get there.

At last, I was starting to see the fruits of my labor after 4 years of hustle.

* * *

On Wednesday, October 3rd, a day I'll always remember, I pulled into the parking lot of my apartment complex preparing to enter my grandmother's apartment after receiving a voicemail message from my mother instructing me to meet her there after I got home from football practice. Exhausted from hellacious conditioning, I did as I was told. I sat down on my grandmother's couch, more comfortable than usual, as if it was anticipating to catch my depleted body.

"Some things have changed in my finances and it's getting too expensive to live up here. We're going to move down south with your grandma in about a month and a half," my mother said with solemnity.

My mother proceeded to tell me more about our situation, the fact she couldn't make ends meet and her concerns that we were going to be evicted from our home. We talked about her fear of us living out of a car and the kindness of her mother, my grandmother, to take us in. It wouldn't be our home — but it would work until we could get things back on track.

"So wait, does this mean we were homeless… again?" I asked trying to process the seriousness of what was transpiring. This situation was eerily similar to something we experienced when I was a mere child.

My mom was quick to point out this was only temporary —
while we may be homeless, this was temporary.

* * *

An army veteran, my mother did not have the opportunity
to attend university at age 18. However, staying true to the
hustler's mentality, she always made a way. Much like myself,
she had aspirations of becoming an entrepreneur. In fact, she
ultimately capitalized on her lived experiences and created
the "Prodigy 2020 Foundation" a non-profit organization
designed to help veterans reintegrate into civilian life using the
four basic squares of life: economic, social, faith, and health.

Our lives paralleled, in this sense, because as she was aiming
to become the first entrepreneur in our family, I was aiming
to be the first one to go to college. Just as she believed in me,
I believed in her. 2013 was supposed to be the year of laying
the framework for the bountiful blessings that we were slated
to receive in 2014.

Life doesn't always go how you expect it to.

* * *

"You'll wrap up here and we'll be moving in with your Grandmother in six weeks."

A month and a half? A MONTH AND A HALF?! How could I possibly move to Georgia during my senior year in high school? Was she forgetting that I needed to get a lot of help from my guidance counselors since I was applying to many elite schools (Ivy League included) and, more selfishly speaking, I would essentially be robbed of the perennial, coveted senior year experience that I was *destined* to have?

I begged and pleaded with her but, as the adult and provider, she ultimately had the final say. November 15th would be my last day in the Chicagoland Area before heading down south. My chest tightened, the lump in my throat expanded exponentially, and I was at a loss for words.

The vision I had for myself heading into my senior year in high school was being shattered and decimated right before my eyes.

I'd gone from nearly being the Homecoming King to a title no one wanted:

Homeless.

∗ ∗ ∗

I didn't know how to break this news to anyone. I have never been the type to divulge bad news simply because I hate the optics of how people can interpret it as me seeking pity; pride and I have a very long and storied history.

Do I send a text? Should I send an email? Should I tell my closest friends what's going on and let them relay the message? Or should I just up and leave school without a trace?

I had no clue.

My football team made it to the first round of the IHSA Class 7A football playoffs. I was out with an injury and was watching helplessly on the sideline as my team struggled.

We lost in the first round.

Just like that, our season was over. Emotions were high after the game simply because the senior class felt as though we had underperformed when it counted most.

Amidst our final goodbyes, in the context of football season, I decided this was the moment that I would let them know I was moving.

Man, was it emotional.

Everyone was surprised that I was leaving so abruptly and,

truthfully, I didn't know how to tell them what the reason was. Was I ashamed?

Unfortunately, I was.

Word got around pretty fast about my situation. Typically, I never shy away from the spotlight. However, as I walked through those halls for what would be the last times, I just wished all eyes would be diverted from me.

Strangely enough, I didn't cry once during this entire ordeal. For the longest time, I thought I was immune to this form of emotional outpour. In fact, on my last day in school, I didn't cry, even when everyone around me was emotional. I simply responded with, "I'll see you soon."

I didn't know how true it was, but I figured I would speak it into existence.

It wasn't until my friends saw me off for my final moment in the Chicagoland Area that I realized the magnitude of the situation. This was it.

I broke down crying. I couldn't control it. Everything in my life was being ripped from me and all I could do was ask God, "Why?"

After I moved down to Georgia, we visited and toured what was to be my new school. I walked into the classroom — my homeroom. It was dark and the furniture looked like it hadn't changed since the 1950s. The desks were covered in graffiti, the floor was dingy, and the lights that hung from the ceiling were flickering.

This was a shock to my system.

As I reviewed the curriculum for the remainder of my senior year, I quickly realized that I'd be learning concepts that I'd previously learned during my freshman or sophomore years — in some cases, things we'd covered in middle school. This was not going to work, especially for a kid who had his heart set on advancing his education beyond what anyone in his family had ever done.

Without getting into too many semantics, I told my school in Illinois the situation. Since they were sympathetic, they let me graduate early. The plan was to treat my time from November of 2013 to August of 2014 as a "gap year" of sorts. I was to continue learning Spanish on my own, learn the rest of calculus 1 on my own, and anything else that would be academically befitting to me on my own.

On my own.

After arriving in Georgia, nearly every aspect of my life had changed. I was sad, mad, frustrated, confused and angry. Anger was my most common emotion and I found myself lashing out at the most random times. Although my anger never turned physical, a lot of the verbal outbursts were either targeted at my mother or at God.

A few weeks earlier, I'd been a potential homecoming king and now I was alone in an unfamiliar land without anyone who I could depend on.

I thought that being in Georgia would be a reclamation of my family identity of sorts since that's where most of my people are from. Instead, my mother and I didn't get any help from our blood and it truly seemed as though they received satisfaction from seeing us down.

Emotionally, I was at one of the lowest points in my life. Looking back now, I realize I was in the early stages of depression. Gone were my friends — a group of young men who had supported one another throughout our youth. I'd never been particularly close to my family growing up and those friends had become my family.

I was feeling alone.

***

I kept checking my email every day, probably about fifty times a day. I was hoping to get an email from my Chicago friends. But more importantly, I was hoping to hear back from the colleges I'd applied to before I was dropped into rural Georgia.

In those six weeks before I left Chicago, with the frantic work of my guidance counselors, I was able to finish three applications for early admissions to some top schools on my list: University of Virginia, Yale University, and the University of Miami. I could see myself at each of these universities and each one represented a potential little piece of hope and optimism while I struggled in my new home.

I knew getting into one of them would mean I could stop worrying and start focusing my head towards the next phase of my life.

And the biggest dream school on the list also happened to guarantee me a full ride if I was accepted: Yale.

I knew that if I was accepted into Yale, it would be the golden ticket needed to get my family out from the trenches we were stuck in. Based on their commitment to giving low income students access, extensive program offerings, and bevy of resources available, I was sold on the idea that this was where

I was *destined* to be. Hell, it was one of the "Big 3" my mother told me I would be attending and I genuinely loved what I knew about the school.

Not to mention, I had an interview with an Alumni Interviewer who said that I was the best applicant he had seen in years and believed Yale would be doing themselves a disservice by not accepting me. If I received the thumbs up from Yale, my mother and I would also be receiving a peace of mind as we could stop worrying because we would know where I'd be spending the next four years of my life.

Finally on December 15th, an email arrived in my inbox with an "@Yale.edu" address. I knew this was the biggie. This was the one that could make this challenging senior year worth it and give me the ability to know — really know — that it had all been worth it. Losing things like watching my friends play sports in front of our entire school, attending prom, experiencing holidays together, senior superlatives, graduating with my best friends, and most importantly, the emotional stability of my mother... all of it.

My heart quickened as I moved the mouse cursor over the email. I wasn't ready to click just yet. I knew what this could do. I knew how it could change my life. While I was terrified to open it, at the same time I was optimistic that this decision would be the pick me up my family and I desperately needed.

I figured God would allow 2013 to end on a positive note considering how quickly the year shifted.

I took a deep breath and clicked.

"Your application has been deferred."

Deferred.

'Okay,' I told myself. Deferred isn't rejected. This is good right? Maybe it just means a couple weeks. It's just deferred. Deferred.

Damn.

This was not what I was looking for; not the relief I wanted. I was without the divine intervention I yearned for and was left to figure out the rest of my college application process by myself with two weeks left before deadlines.

On my own.

* * *

Could you imagine applying to 10+ schools in the span of 2ish weeks without anyone's help?

Hectic.

Raw.

Trying.

All of these words describe that 2-week period. In retrospect, I must say that in that period, I created some of my most unfiltered writing to date simply because I wanted to capture my emotional state not because I wanted the reader to necessarily experience what I was feeling, but rather to introduce them to my world.

* * *

Later on in January, I received a notification email from the University of Virginia. I really didn't know what to expect... so I expected the worst. UVA was such a hard school to get into, especially as an out of state student, and I just wasn't as competitive of an applicant as I originally thought. I'd been in this situation before. I wasn't new to it. Whatever, I didn't really even want to go to UVA anyways.

"Congratulations!"

LET'S GET IT!

I screamed at the seat of the computer. I was finally accepted into a college—a great one at that. I'm still grateful to UVA for that acceptance as it wasn't just a mere acceptance; it was literally the turning point for me. After this notification, I suddenly had a little more pep in my step; I felt more compelled to leave my bed and go outside while beginning to actively seek jobs in order to contribute financially at home. This very acceptance saved me from the pits of depression, simply put.

However, I still had to wait until March to truly see where my future was. My top choice was Yale and I didn't know how UVA's financial aid would be considering it is a public institution. So many questions… and not enough answers.

All I could do was wait.

* * *

Sitting there alone in Georgia for nearly four months wasn't doing me any good. I realized I needed to stop fixating on college application decisions and see my friends. Fortunately, I saved up enough money at my job at the local Dairy Queen to not only take care of bills at home, but also to visit my friends in Illinois. My mother understood and encouraged me to do it.

Welcome home.

As I stepped off the plane, I knew I would be expecting emailed decisions from at least six more schools — and these were the remaining top choices on my list: four from the Ivys, George-town and Duke, what some people called two of the new Ivys. There was a little bit of pressure off of me — I'd already gotten word that I'd been admitted to the University of Virginia. While it wasn't my top choice, it was hard to be frustrated about getting into an incredible school like UVA.

I'd just had my heart set on proving everyone wrong by getting into one of my top 6 — Yale, Columbia, Brown, University of Pennsylvania, Duke, and Georgetown. That would prove to everyone that this crazy turn of events that had led me from stability and a network of people supporting me in Chicago to sitting alone in Georgia did not get the best of nor hindered me from the path my mother and I envisioned for myself since I was a child.

As I stepped off the plane and my friends picked me up from the airport, I did everything I could do to avoid running to a computer to open my email. I knew there could be emails arriving with the news I was anxiously waiting for. Finally, after spending the afternoon with my friends, catching up and finally feeling home again, I had a free moment alone to open my email.

Although I was bitter about the college application decisions, I wasn't really surprised. Although my GPA and class rank were gaudy, my test scores were my biggest inhibitors and I really didn't know if my personal story could make up for such a large deficit. Although I was confident I could make it anywhere if a school decided to take a chance on me, I was a bad test taker and most of these schools aren't willing to take that chance—especially since retention and 4-year graduation rates are so important to them.

I called my mom after opening the five new emails in my inbox.

"What's the news?"

"0 for 5, I said. Yeah, it didn't really work out well but it's whatever," I offered trying to hide my disappointment. "I'll be at UVA in the fall so it's all good."

"Wait, I thought you said there were six more schools you were waiting on?" she replied offering a hopeful reply.

"Oh, yeah well those are all the ones with electronic notifications. Georgetown doesn't do electronic notifications. The mail decision should be there in the next week and you can open it. Don't expect anything from it though because it's likely that I didn't get in considering I couldn't even get into any of these others."

"Oh... okay." I heard the disheartenment in her voice. No mom wants their kid disappointed. I went to bed that night trying not to blame all the turmoil we'd been through for this result.

But it was hard; I felt like it had.

The next morning, my cell phone buzzed. It was my mom.

"Hey mom, don't worry I'm okay," I said trying to predict the reason for her call.

"MY BABY GOT INTO GEORGETOWN!" she exclaimed, crying through the phone.

#TheDecision

A smile crept across my face.

I was so sure that I would be attending UVA in the fall and this acceptance switched the whole game up for me. I had the opportunity to attend college in Washington, D.C., our nation's capital, while also getting the chance to be there for the 2016 election. D.C. seemed far more attractive than Charlottesville, admittedly so, and began to win me over.

I received my financial aid from Georgetown...

Damn near a full ride.

2014 started out rough but started to shift in a big way.

Although it didn't come when I wanted it to, it came right on time.

Divine Intervention.

★ ★ ★

I'd made it.

And yet the reality of my situation was apparent. Although this was a triumphant moment for my mother and I, the state of euphoria was short lived as I had to begin thinking about next steps. As the materials from Georgetown arrived, including a list of 'pre-reading' that would have taken me a year to read thoroughly, I quickly felt overwhelmed.

I'd been a great student — one of the best — at my public high school. I worked hard and every moment of free time was spent studying, working and keeping on track while many of my peers were out with friends.

Georgetown was now my new address.

And yet, I was enrolling into one of the most elite schools in the country at a serious disadvantage. The public school

I went to paled in comparison to the elite boarding schools many of my peers would be coming from. In many ways, it was like comparing the school in Georgia I had avoided to my Chicago-area high school. I was no longer the kid who my classmates looked up to in order to show them the way... I was the kid they might have looked at and felt sorry for.

To make matters worse, this opportunity was the blessing my family and I had been waiting for since my adolescence and if I failed, there was essentially no hope; I had no safety net.

Had I made a mistake taking on a challenge this big? Just five months earlier my mom and I had experienced homelessness and a move to rural Georgia.

Now I was joining an institution where more than half of my classmates had graduated as first, second or third in their high school class. Half.

I wasn't going to let that get in my way. I'd accomplished too much already.

I had to win.

Upon recognizing that academic excellence was the only way for me to get my family out of a cycle of generational poverty and achieve upward social mobility, I realized I had no other choice but to win at college.

I didn't have the advantages of boarding school education, tutors, nor the best pedigree of my secondary institution. But I did have something most of my peers didn't: everything to lose.

I had no choice but to make it work. And so I set out to do whatever it took.

I sat down in my room and began to read everything I could — every article, every expert interview, every book. My goal was to learn every single advantage I could find — all above board and legit — but all designed to ensure I didn't get behind.

I planned to "hack" college.

Hack: strategically playing the hand you've been dealt in order to out-perform your peers while still enjoying the experience.

Without any margin for error, in terms of academics, my plan even exceeded my personal goals.

Yes, I am winning.

In 4 semesters at Georgetown, I've made the Dean's List every semester (maintained at least a 3.5 GPA in a given semester) while achieving Second Honors the semester in which this book was written (maintained at least a 3.7 GPA in a given semester). In addition, I have held numerous leadership positions, interned with the DC Public School system, and have recently accepted an offer to intern with Google in the summer of 2017.

Yes, you can look at me as a kid from public schools, who moved around, and was one of the only ever in his family to go to college. Yes, I came from an impoverished background living in a single parent home, homeless as a child, and nearly homeless during my senior year. All of those are true.

Or you could see me as the kid who is living his dream, who has outperformed many of his boarding school-educated classmates, and who will be interning at one of the premier and most competitive companies in America all because he figured out what you should and should not do in college.

The goal of this book will be to lay out the framework and guiding principles of my journey and success in a manner that is easily understandable for the purpose of implementation into your own repertoire so that you, too, can hack college.

HOW YOU HACK COLLEGE:

- What you DO NOT need to do, stress or worry about (lots of people tell you these things matter, but based on my research, study and own experiences, they don't matter or really move the needle):
  - Sleep Less
  - Cram Study
  - Over Study
  - Over-Commit Yourself
  - Allow External Parties/Pressures Dictate Your Choices
- What you DO need to do: ATTEND
  - **A**ttitude. You need to go in with a chip on your shoulder but not the feeling like you are at a disadvantage. You deserve success just as much as anyone else (Ch. 1)
  - **T**arget. Students who excel know their target. What are your skills and interests? (Ch. 2) What is your ultimate aim from college and why are you seeking this journey? (Ch. 3)
  - **T**ime. Limit extra curriculars and time wasters (Ch. 4) and build a time management system that optimizes Sleep, Study & Exercise. (Ch. 5)
  - **E**fficiency. Develop your unfair advantage — a way to focus on what really matters. Make the most out of your time allotted and stay on track. (Ch. 6)
  - i**N**-class participation. A great way to show professors that you care about the material is by becoming an active contributor to the class discussion. (Ch. 7)
  - **D**ue diligence. Follow up with your professors in their

office hours and ensure that you've advocated yourself to the best of your ability through getting to know them, asking questions, and being likable. (Ch.8)

As most research would suggest, I should not be in the position that I'm in today or the positions that I will be in the future... and yet I'm still here.

This wasn't achieved overnight. This was a process I had to teach myself predicated on the mere fact that I had no choice but to win.

And I'm sharing it.

I invite you all to join me on my journey of hacking college.

PART 1

DEEP INTROSPECTION

CHAPTER 1

SECONDARY SCHOOLING

———

WHAT YOU'LL LEARN:

- The circumstances that led to me reflecting on my high school education.
- Examples of students from high-income backgrounds and elite schools academically thriving as well as academically underperforming.
- Examples of students from low-income backgrounds and struggling schools academically thriving as well as academically underperforming.

Georgetown University. Hoya Saxa.

I still couldn't believe it. A school of such caliber that had access to power and resources beyond my conceivable imagination really chose me.

Suddenly, song lyrics meant that much more.

"Quantum physics could never show you the world I was in," Kendrick Lamar rapped on his verse on "Nosetalgia".

How could anyone possibly understand my world? Whenever I tried to reach out to my friends to talk and/or vent about what my mother and I had been through in the past 6 months, everyone was sympathetic, but no one really understood what my emotions were or what it was truly like to spend a day in my shoes; empathy was emphatically absent.

With the addition of the acceptance letter, although I was eternally grateful, I realized my world got immensely more complicated. I was slated to attend one of the most prestigious universities in the world on a full ride via financial aid while my mother would remain in Georgia living in public housing. Although I didn't know what "survivor's remorse" was at that time, I was certainly feeling it before I even touched down in D.C.

"Damn right I like the life I live because I went from negative to positive." – The Notorious B.I.G. from his smash hit, "Juicy".

Yes, although there was confliction, there was no doubt in my mind that things weren't turning around. 8-months prior, my future was in peril. The fruits of my labor were on the brink of not becoming actualized. So many trials and tribulations were facing us, and we almost waved the white flag.

But we didn't. We chose to fight, and I thank God every day for giving us the willpower to do so and planting a seed of hope within us.

With this sense of hope, I found myself with a renewed sense of excitement for the next chapter of my life. As a result, I researched everything I could about Georgetown. I tried to research the types of professors that were currently teaching, different tracks of study that I might want to pursue, and the types of students that would encompass the rest of the Class of 2018.

Intimidated.

That's the only word that could aptly described how I felt after researching a good amount of student profiles.

As with most universities, a class Facebook page was made months before orientation in order to give students an opportunity to connect with each other and get to know each other a little bit better. Out of genuine curiosity, I looked at a number of profiles to gain more insight about them.

I knew that my peers would be "elite" but I never really knew what "elite" fully encompassed.

To my surprise, I found a reoccurring theme amongst the students on this page. They were research winners of world-renowned competitions; I never even knew about these opportunities growing up.

They were Gates Millennium Scholars, Coca Cola Scholarship recipients, and every other big name scholarship you can think of under the sun; I didn't win any scholarships coming out of high school. If it wasn't for financial aid, I wouldn't be here today.

"What schools are producing these types of students?" I wondered.

Thy were coming from Exeter Academy, Milton Academy, college preparatory schools, private schools, and the best public schools.

Although I was thankful for what my high school had done for me, I couldn't help but hold resentment for the fact that I didn't think it prepared me for a school like Georgetown, when juxtaposed with some of my peers.

I thought I had known so much about the academic world but after my research, I was certain that my exposure had been reduced to a marginal fraction of what is actually out there.

I'm not the type to place blame easily, but I couldn't help but think:

Did my public school education fail me?

* * *

ATTITUDE.T.T.E.N.D.

Without a doubt,

Before even getting into the derivations for my success at Georgetown, I believe it's imperative to dive further into the secondary education that I was exposed to. Admittedly, I went to a pretty good public school. However, as a low-income student, I was worried about how I would fare against my peers considering Georgetown has pretty good placement amongst the elite high schools.

From my initial understanding, I assumed that the positive correlation between wealth & rigor of high school and academic success in college was set in stone. Although I concede that there are certainly general trends and indicators among the highest academically achieving students (like wealth and rigor of high school), this does not mean this is guaranteed to determine your collegiate experience.

Essentially, just because you come from one of the elite boarding schools and are in the upper middle class does not mean you are destined to excel in college. On the same accord, just because you come from a failing school district and are classified as a low-income student does not mean you are destined to under-perform and drop out of school. Don't believe me? Let's examine my evidence then.

I interviewed a wide variety of individuals for this book so that instead of letting my own implicit biases dictate the advisory content, I'd have empirical evidence guiding you to the promised land that is academic excellence. With that being said, one of the individuals that I interviewed early on was Edgar Milton, currently a senior at Georgetown. Edgar went to an elite boarding school in the Northeast, comes from an affluent background, believes that the high school he went to was more academically rigorous than Georgetown, and has been able to make at least the Dean's List (at least a 3.5 in a given semester) every semester of his undergraduate career.

Upon evaluating his tangible measurables, it appears that his path to academic success was sort of a given right? Based on his background and inherent level of privilege, the only reason he would fail is because he chose to, right? Yes, his privilege has played a role in his academic success thus far but to be honest, Edgar works extremely hard. Some of the biggest determinants in why he's done exceptionally well is because he is aware of his strengths and weakness, is thorough in terms of his preparation and approach for every class, and, above all else, recognizes that doing well academically will help him achieve many of his goals so, naturally, he places academics as a priority.

As I've said before, wealth and rigor of high school are not the end-all-be-all when it comes to academic success. I also interviewed Michelle Camper, currently a junior at Georgetown. Michelle comes from an upper-middle class, two-parent household and also attended an academically rigorous private school. Just like Edgar, she comes from a privileged background. However, her academic performance differs vastly from Edgar. She has yet to make the Dean's List and, admittedly, needs to see a stark improvement in her academics if she is to remain on track for her desired career.

Although, in theory, she was destined for academic success, she has had her fair share of challenges. For example, she is pursuing a major in a field in which she is not naturally good at, stretches herself thin (in terms of extracurricular activities), and also does not study as much as she should be.

I've been talking a lot about some of my upper-middle class peers; I now want to shift the focus to students that are on the lower end of the socioeconomic totem pole. Emmanuel Joubie is currently a sophomore at Georgetown coming from a single-parent, low-income household. When asked about how well his school prepared him for the academic rigor of Georgetown, he responded with, "Don't get me wrong, I love my school and am thankful I had the opportunity to go there. But when it comes down to how well it prepared me academically? Nah man, I was not prepared at all."

With me showing that extraction from my interview with him, one might expect him to have been having a rough time adjusting to the rigorous Georgetown climate. To the contrary; Emmanuel has had an impressive track record thus far including making the Dean's List every semester, finding enjoyment and making direct impact in the organizations that he is a part of, interned with the Department of Education, and is set to intern with a Tech company this summer!

If I had to liken him to anyone, it would be Edgar. Although they have entered Georgetown from vastly different places of privilege, their approach to college has been nearly identical. As a result, they've both ascertained levels of academic success that many would be envious of. With that being said, although their personal backgrounds could not be more dissimilar, the common thread between them is evident: the silver lining of hustle.

Albert is an example of someone who comes from a low-income background that is struggling thus far in his undergraduate experience. Unfortunately, it appears as though that nothing he does is working. Georgetown seems to be an extremely hard academic environment for him as he is not experiencing academic success to the degree that he would like.

At this point, you might be curious as to why I brought Edgar, Michelle, Emmanuel and Albert into the mix. Well, if you break it down by socioeconomic class, Edgar and Michelle are grouped together while Emmanuel and Albert are grouped together. On the upper-middle class spectrum, I provided examples of both someone thriving and another facing a multitude of academic challenges. On the low-income side, I also provided an example of someone academically succeeding despite the barriers he faces and another who's barriers are in fact inhibiting his academic performance.

Therefore, we see that that although wealth and rigor of high school may be *contributing* factors, they are not *definite* factors, in terms of predicting your college success.

In fact, research suggests that other factors have just as much as influence when it comes to predicting your collegiate success including social relationships, stress levels, curiosity, EQ (Emotional Intelligence), your family, class times, fitness, sleep, successful college athletics, and health (as pulled from onlineuniversities.com)

Don't leave factors that are out of your control, such as socio-economic class and type of secondary school, determine who you are destined to be. Instead, focus on what you can control with a great starting point being your attitude.

To put yourself in the frame of thought where nothing is given and everything is earned, you must come in with a gritty mentality of not being denied.

When on the road to academic excellence, you must adopt the mentality of the underdog; in essence, you must scrap and fight for every grade, leadership position—anything you are striving for.

"You can't mean everything, right Adrian?"

Yes, everything. Academic greatness is a lot more likely if you fight for everything. It really just comes down to how bad you want it.

If you played competitive sports at one point, you probably remember your coach questioning your passion or will to win when it came down to conditioning drills in practice. Those that showed more dedication typically spent longer hours in the gym, made sure to do every rep of a workout/drill, and overall tried their hardest to ensure they did the little things right.

Therefore, you must apply that same concept to wanting to do well in college. You've got to fight for everything.

Without a doubt, if I had to point to one factor that has played in my academic success in high school and college, it would be sheer grit. Hell, I had grit before I even knew what the word was (in large part due to my childhood and environment).

Early on, I was always competitive when it came to academics. I always yearned to be the best and outperform my "smarter" peers. I use "smarter" in quotations because I was usually the only Black kid in my predominantly White advanced classes and I always had to work twice as hard to get the same recognition as my White counterparts. Because of this racialized environment and the barriers I had to overcome due to my skin color, outperforming my peers was always that much more meaningful.

It wasn't easy, however. Classes were hard (and are still hard) for me. Some of my peers didn't even have to study for tests in order to do well. By all statistical measures, I shouldn't have graduated in the 20th of 595 kids.

Where my peers had me beat in natural intellect I made up for with pure grit and sheer heart.

Win from within. Worry about the things that you can control and everything will take care of itself.

* * *

FOOD FOR THOUGHT

If you, like me, want to understand your competition to the best of your capabilities and not get blindsided after stepping on campus, below you will find a couple of tips to understand both the type of school system from which you come from in addition to understanding what backgrounds your peers may be coming from as well.

America was built on capitalism and college is fueled by competition. Know your environment.

For The High School You Went To:

- Look up rankings, if possible, to see where your school ranks in the state. If successful, take this a step further and try to discover your school's national ranking.
- Have honest and open conversations with different administrators from your school and get their thoughts on where they think the school is excelling versus where they feel as though the school needs to improve. Document both of these.
  - The purpose for documenting both is to match against other schools. For example, your school might not offer study abroad programs. Although you may not understand the benefit of study abroad, research school districts that

offer it, explore their rational for why it's important, then understand how some of your peers may have a leg up on you in this regard.

- Discover what your high school's graduation rate is.
- Discover what the placement of graduates from your school looks like in regards to the workforce, 4-year university, trade school, the military, etc.

For The High Schools Your Peers In College Went To:

- Check on your university website to see where most students are coming from. If it's a state school, you know that most of the students will be in state, thus allowing you to hone in on your research thereafter. If it's a private university with a large endowment, chances are they are attracting a variety of different students from across the globe, thus meaning your research will be expanded.
- Most universities offer Facebook groups for admitted students into their respective years. This will give you first hand insight into the type of students that will be attending your university due to the nature of how much information people typically share on social media.
  - Don't try to document every single school you see. Look for general trends such as seeing students attending public schools vs students attending private schools vs students attending boarding school. Discovering these general trends

allow you to come up with pretty good "guestimations", as far as what type of schools your peers are coming from.

If you don't take anything else away from this book, know this: college is up for grabs! At the end of the day, the skills that the most successful collegiate students are utilizing can be applied to anyone in any place despite your background! Correlation does not always dictate causation; the next couple of chapters are designed to equip you with premium strategic knowledge that will allow you to have complete autonomy over your collegiate experience and not let wealth or rigor of your high school determine your aptitude for academic success.

CHAPTER 2

KNOWING YOUR STRENGTHS, WEAKNESSES, AND PASSIONS

———

WHAT YOU'LL LEARN

- The importance of targeting your specific strengths, weaknesses, and passions.
- Methodologies I used to discover mine.
- My recommendations for the different resources and methodologies you can utilize to discover yours.

Before the commencement of my inaugural year at Georgetown, before I even moved into my freshman year dorm, I had a long, honest conversation with myself. About a month before my departure date, I had a dream that on my first report card from Georgetown and the grades I received were a mixture of C's and D+'s.

As you can probably tell, I take my grades very seriously. As a result of said dream, I woke up in a panic. Never before had I received a C, let alone a D, on a report card and the mere thought of it sent me into a frenzy. When I woke up, many of my insecurities started reemerging. Was I good enough? Did Georgetown make a mistake accepting me?

The imposter syndrome was real.

In need of inspiration, I found it in an unlikely source: my reflection in my bathroom mirror. As I was brushing my teeth in the morning, I stopped what I was doing and had an honest conversation with myself.

"Okay Adrian, you're smart, yeah, but it's not like you were a National Merit Scholar. Hell, you weren't even the salutatorian of your class."

"Sure, your mother supports you like no other and gives you her unconditional love, but it might pale in comparison to the breadth of resources that some of your peers from Exeter are bringing with them to college."

Okay. Okay.

"Although those things are true, you have defied insurmountable odds to get to this point, so this is nothing new. Think about it, when it looked like you were down for the count, you always responded. What did you respond with?"

Strategy. In the face of adversity, I always had a strategy.

"There you go. Now we're getting somewhere. Grit, resiliency, and determination is the name of the collegiate game. Let's figure it out."

* * *

A.TARGET.T.E.N.D.

For many of us, high school was a time for great exploration. Whether this was spiritual exploration, academic exploration, or social exploration, 4 years in high school allowed us to discover different realms and traits of our person. With that being said, understanding your academic strengths, weaknesses, and passions will be imperative to your overall success on the collegiate level. Therefore, you will need to reflect on your secondary schooling and understand what you're bringing to the table

When determining what your own strengths and weaknesses are, it is also important to note the inherent level of subjectivity that goes into this process of discernment. Therefore, it's important to understand what this book defines as an academic strength.

As a general rule of thumb, if you've been able to routinely get B's or higher in a specific academic discourse, like in the maths or sciences, then I would say that, most likely, these are where your academic strengths lie. Ideally, you would have been able to take the highest course offerings at your school including Honors, Advanced Placement, and International Baccalaureate.

However, I understand that not everyone reading this book was able to take those sorts of classes whether it was due to institutional barriers (schools not offering that specific coursework) or not taking the classes because you and your family decided it was not the best for you at that time.

After heavily considering the aforementioned variables, I have determined that the above rule of thumb still applies but requires a higher degree of vigilance. In essence, you will most likely know your academic strengths as a result of said rule but be aware of the rule not being completely conclusive while also being flexible enough to be willing to find your academic strengths again (if need be).

At this point, you might be thinking, "I don't really know what my academic strengths are. How am I supposed to figure that out?"

Well, I'm glad you asked! Let's talk about it:

HOW I DID IT: EXAMINING EASY VS. HARD CLASSES

For one, I think a great place to go is your report cards. All you need to do is quickly reflect on the types of classes you took in high school and see if your best grades are concentrated in specific courses and subjects. See if there's any correlations between the types of courses that you were getting mostly A's and B's in a semester (or quarter). This allows you to compartmentalize your strengths by academic subject which will, in turn, better prepare you to understand your academic limitations (if there are any) and how this coincides with university obligations such as a core curriculum that requires you to take multiple classes in subjects that you are generally weaker in.

However, there needs to be caution when undergoing this process of determination. For instance, just because you got an A in a class doesn't mean that it's constituted as a strength. The process of discerning that includes understanding if the class was a "hard" class or if it was relatively "easy." I would constitute an easy class as one where the teachers give you lots of extra credit and created an environment in which it was hard to fail essentially. A hard class might look like multiple students struggling through the duration of the course, average tests grades being abysmal, or the teacher outright saying they believe in "grade deflation."

The components of understanding where your strengths are

also include getting a variety of different perspectives from faculty and friends. If you're coming fresh out of high school, I would talk to your teachers that you've taken (at least one in every subject) and see see what their vantage points were, as far as your contributions to the class, them seeing you in a future career related to that subject, and things of that nature.

This concept is reminiscent of W.E.B. DuBois' term "Double Consciousness." As written in his book, *The Souls of Black Folk,* the term refers to the, "This sense of always looking at one's self through the eyes of others, of measuring one's soul by the tape of a world that looks on in amused contempt and pity. One ever feels his two-ness, —an American, a Negro; two souls, two thoughts, two unreconciled strivings; two warring ideals in one dark body, whose dogged strength alone keeps it from being torn asunder."

Therefore, you must feel the two-ness in the context of secondary education. In one regard, you must hypothesize what your academic strengths are based on the material on which you have been assessed. In another regard, you must hypothesize what your educators deem as your academic strengths based on them seeing raw knack for the course material, your performance on assessments, participation in class, and their vision for you in that field (if they have any). Then take the latter concept a step further by actually getting feedback from your educators so you don't make false assumptions about your strengths and weaknesses.

Therefore, it's a mixture of understanding internally what you've done well in verses also making sure you get that outside perspective and then, from there, utilizing those two [sometimes] different perspectives in order to perform logical deductive reasoning and coming to your own rational conclusion about what your strengths and weaknesses are.

HOW I DID IT: IDENTIFYING MY INTEREST/PASSIONS

Author's note: I am a proponent of interest potentially leading to developing one's passion. As a result, I will be citing research on interest even though this section is predicated on identifying passions.

Broadly speaking, it is important to understand what you genuinely enjoy doing in terms of your interests and passions. Once you understand this framework, you should then cross reference this with the academic disciplines available to you at any of the universities that you are interested in.

For example, if you genuinely enjoy writing in your spare time, you might want to consider being an English major. Or if you work very well with your hands and have a knack for design, spatial intelligence, and the ability to think qualitatively, you may want to consider a technical field, potentially engineering.

In addition, research suggests that if you are enrolled in coursework that you are genuinely interested in or genuinely enjoy, the chances are that you'll perform better in these courses as opposed to courses where you have no interest or passion for the material.

Furthermore, Annie Murphy Paul, the author of, *"Brilliant: The New Science of Smart"*, wrote, "In fact, scientists have shown that passionate interests can even allow people to overcome academic difficulties or perceptual disabilities. One study found that students who scored poorly on achievement tests but had well-developed interests in reading or mathematics were more likely to engage with the meaning of textual passages or math problems than were peers with high scores but no such interests. Another study, of prominent academics and Nobel Laureates who struggled with dyslexia, found that they were able to persist in their efforts to read because they were motivated to explore an early and ardent interest."

Great. Now you all know the importance of taking classes that align with your interests or passions!

This is only half the battle, however. Because many schools have a mission to ensure their students are well rounded, many universities offer core curriculums; Georgetown has a commitment to "educate the whole person" stemming from the institution's jesuit values. This translates to one thing:

I've had to take so many classes that *I didn't like*. At all.

Micro and Macro Econ, Spanish, History, etc. In fact, 80% of my lowest final grades come from classes that were core requirements. Therefore, if you're a university student that has to deal with a core requirement, this next point is for you:

"What happens if I have to take classes that I have no interest?

In my opinion, you have two options. For one, you could just weather the storm, quite frankly. The second option consists of creating a pseudo interest in the class yourself.

Following the same train of thought as the "pulling yourself up by the bootstraps" mentality, you have the option of incorporating that very same framework into the classes that do not interest you in the slightest bit. When adopting this mentality, you must recognize the challenges that are in your way while still aiming to overcome the odds by any means necessary with minimal help along the way.

In my opinion, adoption of this mentality makes sense in theory but, in reality, one may find it more difficult than previously imagined. Common results of this adoption can include eventually losing motivation for wanting to do well in the class in addition to not performing as well as one would like to. With that being said, I am not really a fan of this approach and see the negatives outweighing the positives simply due to how easy it is to fall into the trap of the aforementioned negatives.

Instead, I would recommend being creative in your approach when trying to make non-interesting classes interesting. In fact, this approach has worked for some of my peers at Georgetown. Edgar is an individual that has ascribed to this mentality and has seemingly reaped the benefits.

Edgar is currently a senior at Georgetown University and has quite the brag sheet. Not only has he held multiple leadership positions on campus and received a job offer after an internship in the summer after his junior year, he also has been on the Dean's List every semester (at least a 3.5) and will be graduating with honors. He concedes that a large part of his academic success comes from his view on classes.

In his opinion, there are three types of classes most students will find themselves taking: 1) classes that they HAVE to take (hard to motivate themselves) 2) classes that they want to take (they're genuinely interested) 3) middle of the road classes.

When taking the classes where he finds it hard to motivate himself, he starts off with the baseline understanding of him needing to do well in the class in order to protect his GPA if no other reason at all. Therefore, he aims to create an aspect of the class that is interesting to him. Whether or not this includes trying to build a personal relationship with the professor or creating fun pneumonic devices to remember different definitions in class, he aims to figure out something that will help entice him to the class, even if it is only for a semester.

Hell, in some cases, he finds himself actually enjoying the class because of the initial predication on pseudo-interest ends up transforming into genuine interest. In the worst cases, he found himself getting good grades in these tough classes and weathering the storm. In either case, he came out on top.

And who wouldn't want that?

WHAT I RECOMMEND YOU DOING: EVERYTHING

From the research I've done and from the personal testimonies I've heard, it's plain to see that one of the differences between students who attend the best of the best high schools have over students who attended less academically rigorous or financially challenged schools is the constant reflection they were required to perform in regards to being pushed to learn and identify their strengths, weaknesses, and passions.

Research on "grit", conducted by Angela Duckworth, has been widely publicized in recent years because of its compelling nature and the thorough documentation of the link to one's overall success. With that being said, it is important to note the relationship between grit and knowing one's self (strengths, weaknesses, etc.). In fact, according to Merriam-Webster's dictionary, grit in the context of behavior refers to the, "firmness of character; indomitable spirit."

In order to achieve a firmness of character or possess an indomitable spirit, one most know the inner-machinations of who they were; one must know their strengths, weaknesses, and passions! Therefore, using the transitive property, introspection leads to development of grit which ultimately leads to one's overall success.

I was the type of student that wasn't exactly aware of where my strengths or passions aligned. I had broad guesses, such as wanting to help people, but was never really pushed to think beyond that. Instead, I was trained to get good grades and get to the next level while neglecting my own process of discovery for my passion and realizing which strengths would be my guiding forces in college. If you're like me, I've got a couple of solutions for you.

These recommendations can be the guiding forces in your process of discovery!

TESTS

Aptitude tests are a great way to identify what some of your strengths and weakness are. While they should never be treated as an end-all-be-all, in terms of sheer definitiveness, they are great to use when you just need something to get the ball rolling.

According to "Careeraddict.com" aptitude tests measure a variety of facets pertinent to someone's identity including abstract reasoning skills, spatial visualization, manual dexterity, numerical aptitude, creative skills, literary skills, organizational skills, leadership skills, spelling, perceptual speed and accuracy, scientific skills, and mechanical reasoning and understanding.

There are many tests you can find online and take from the comfort of your own home. Here are a couple you could find with a simple Google search:

RSWAT: RichardStep Strengths Aptitude Test (Free)

123 Test: Strengths and Weaknesses Test (Free)

Aptitude tests have long been used to help employers predict the success of their future employees and I know this same concept can be transported from the professional world and applied to a collegiate setting.

You can also take tests that help you determine what your

college major should be. If you, like me, were completely clueless about what to major in, this could be a great first place to start.

This is one of my favorite methodologies because you are directly going to the the people that knew you best during your high school experience. The key to ensuring this methodology works is by getting input from those that not only raised you, but those that were able to watch your academic progress closely.

- Start with parents. Since they brought you into this world, they can help you discover different facets to yourself, including strengths and weaknesses, before you are even able to discover them.
- Teachers are a great next step. Ensure that you're not just picking your favorite teachers, but teachers that can really attest to your academic performance and really know who you are as a person.
    - This type of interaction is two-fold in its benefits as it not only helps you understand your strengths and weaknesses, but also allows the teacher to reflect deeply on you as an individual, your relationship with them, and can result in you obtaining a professional mentor or someone willing to write a letter of recommendation.
- Guidance counselors can also be very effective. If you were

fortunate enough to attend a school with enough qualified guidance counselors for the school's population of students, utilize them to help you discover your strengths, weaknesses, and passions. While it is their job, they also genuinely enjoy helping students become the truest forms of their authentic selves.

Between the aforementioned tests and personal interviews you could conduct, I have no doubt that you will be able to develop a better idea of what your strengths, weaknesses, and passions are. Using a conglomeration of the proposed methodologies will put you in a great position in terms of self-discovery.

RECAP

- Self-Discovery of strengths, weaknesses, and passions → a development of behavioral grit → an increase in one's overall success.
- In order to begin this process of discovery, you have a couple of options:
  - Tests
    - Aptitude tests that you can find online
    - Online tests that help you determine what your major in college should be
  - Personal Interviews w/
    - Parents
    - Teachers

- Guidance counselors
  - ▶ Sample Questions:
    - ▷ What do you think I'm naturally good at?
    - ▷ What are some of the best qualities about me?
    - ▷ Am I more type-A or type-B?
    - ▷ Am I more of a qualitative or quantitive thinker?
    - ▷ When I talk, do people listen?

CHAPTER 3

PARADIGM OF LEARNING

WHAT YOU'LL LEARN

- The importance of self-reflection and understanding why you decided to embark on a collegiate journey.
- Self-autonomy is not only imperative to your success in college, but your success in life.
- Once your purpose is identified, goal setting becomes more attainable and exponentially increases your chances of collegiate success.

I'll always remember the day my mother dropped me off for good at Georgetown. We were up the previous night making the 8+ hour trek from Georgia to DC. With bags under my eyes and exhaustion subduing me, we unpacked everything from the car and proceeded to get my room together.

Darnall Hall, also known as the the third worst ranked dormitory in the country at that time, was my assignment for the 2014-2015 school year. Known for its small rooms, rats, and inhospitable living conditions, I was praying for the best but still preparing for the worst.

"Wow! This room is so nice! You and your roommate have got so much space! This is definitely a step up from some of the other rooms I've seen." -My mother.

Her radiant aura of positivity is exactly what I needed at that time. We took our time unloading my suitcase and organizing my room in a neat and strategic manner, savoring every bit of what would be our last moments together for quite some time.

"I'm really proud of you, sugar foot." I normally detest when my mother calls me by her nicknames, but considering these were our final moments, I let it rock. "You've overcome a lot to get to this point and I think that speaks volume as to the type of individual you are. With that being said, you've gotten this far and the real work starts now. You owe it to yourself, and nobody else, to reap the benefits of your labor."

As we walked outside, the sky was gray and I could hear faint thunder in the back. This was it. My heart was racing because I imagined in my head how this moment would play out. I thought that my mom might start crying hysterically because it was just she and I for the past 18 years and now her only son was leaving the nest.

I even thought that I would start balling because she was my biggest supporter for years and I felt guilty about leaving her in the "projects" in Georgia while I was attending such an elite university. The following shocked me:

"Alright, give me a hug sugar bear!" she said while embracing me for a hug. "I'm not really going to do the whole getting emotional thing. This is what we've been fighting for your entire life. You've got work to do; I'll see you in November for Thanksgiving. Love you." I couldn't even get any words out; I didn't know what to say.

As she released her embrace, she swiftly got in her car and drove away.

This was really it. Growing up, all I ever asked for was an opportunity to uplift my family from the cycle of generational poverty; this was my first step in taking that opportunity and "win."

But on that same accord, given the research I saw on students from similar backgrounds as I, there was a strong likelihood that I would "lose."

And if I lost, there was no hope for my family.

College was literally a luxury for most of my peers and at the age of 18, I felt as though it was my family's livelihood; this was my "why" and whether I liked it or not, I had to finally own it.

Could you imagine having that weight on your shoulders at that age?

* * *

A.TARGET.T.E.N.D.

I think that the decision to attend college is very personal and is all dependent on whatever you want as an individual. With that being said, don't enter college just because your parents say that you need to or feeling as though the system is forcing you into a specific "track."

Rather, I would suggest that before enrolling, you should try to understand what your reasons are for matriculating and wanting to do well in college because if you let others dictate your future, in that sense, it's going to be an uphill battle no matter what you're trying to do.

If you are being told that a successful collegiate experience is determined by several key aspects such as getting good grades, solidifying top internships, or making a lot of connections for your social network and your heart is not truly in these things, you are putting yourself in a position for failure, quite frankly.

Even some people here at Georgetown are in fields that they are not particularly passionate about simply because of expectations from third parties such as friends, family, and even society in some cases. For example, I have many friends that are sticking it out in the pre-med field just because their parents want them to be a doctor while they're not passionate nor doing well in the field.

Between this lack of passion and raw talent for the subject material, their GPA is taking a hit, thus putting them in hard positions, in regards to pivoting to other courses of studies or career paths. The same concept can also be applied to my friends in the business school who feel as though the next stepping stone in their life is investment banking as opposed to their true passion that lies within grassroots organizing.

I've also come across some people that are just not that into a traditional college experience in the sense of a four-year university or feel as though these types of schools aren't going to truly utilize their talents and interests. They would rather go to a trade school or just jump straight into the workforce as they don't really have a grand vision for becoming like a CEO, in a traditional sense, since they know that most likely they are going to need an undergraduate degree, potentially an MBA, and so on and so forth.

Therefore, they would rather pursue their own ventures or endeavors and whatnot so at that point they are only meeting their own needs and not living up to the expectations of others.

All in all, I have definitely seen a couple of examples where people are just going to a four year university for what I would call "wrong" reasons. Basically, I define wrong reasons as any reason besides what you want to do for yourself. As you would expect, a "right" reason is essentially any reason that allows you to remain genuine and authentic to who you are.

* * *

For the most part, in my research, I've seen a high degree of variability of derivation for why students want to enroll in college. For some top-performing college students, they say that their motivations are because they want to ensure that they're making the most of the parent's investment.

Others have said that they want to make sure that they can be in a position to give back to their family while some others said that they just enjoy learning. All in all, I've been able to see a huge spectrum, in terms of the different thought processes for why someone would want to enter college and why they want to do well on college.

For what it's worth, I think that if you look at something like college, it's very hard to say "I made it here on my own." I think most people would agree with that assertion. Therefore, I would challenge you, as the reader, to look at the different stakeholders involved in your success and whatnot. You need to identify those that have helped you along your journey because, in my opinion, college is a blessing. Therefore, you must recognize those that helped you ascertain said blessing.

This is a great reflective tool that can be used to show gratitude—an act that can work wonders for your own personal well-being. Studies show that if you show gratitude, not only does this affect the stakeholders and give them a source of feeling good and accomplishment about you expressing your gratitude, but you also feel better as well.

The real question comes down to how the stakeholders will play into the goals that you have for yourself. I am a strong proponent of taking heed to their input and advice because they obviously care about you. However, you must make this decision for yourself and leave the final decision and final say to be yours and no one else's, even if they played a huge role in your life to get you this far.

* * *

As I was interviewing, I was fortunate enough to interview someone named John, a recent graduate of Georgetown who graduated with a 3.9 GPA and currently works at one of the top consulting firms. In this interview, we talked a little bit about how his expectations aligned with his parents goals for what his Georgetown experience should bring about (employment, connections, professional growth, etc).

In addition, this was also an instance of him understanding the stakeholders that were involved in his success, listening to their advice, deciding how it fits into the framework of his vision for life, and not wanting to waste their money while still wanting to make them proud in that regard. Therefore, he used a reverse engineering train of thought.

More specifically, he knew that making them proud translated to doing well in school, getting high level internships, and also getting a job after graduation so he can actually monetarily repay their investment theoretically. He also decided that all of those things were what he wanted out of his collegiate experience for himself, so it ended up working out.

Above all else, I definitely wanted to show a specific vantage point for why someone might want to attain high academic success. In my opinion, he's the standard in the sense of his parents playing pivotal roles in helping him get to a successful point and wanting to make them proud through academics, getting a job so that he can contribute in the repayment of their loans, and so on and so forth.

John's motivation differed from someone else that I interviewed—Edgar. Under my impression, although he understood that college could be a great time for experiential learning and maximum academic growth, it seemed as though all of that would be to no avail unless he was able to secure post-graduate employment.

Therefore, his time at college has been spent with this in the back of his mind as this was his ultimate goal. In order to provide a little more background on Edgar, he is a current senior at Georgetown that is also in the top of his class and has received a post-graduate employment opportunity.

Although John and Edgar had 2 different approaches, I think there are a lot of key takeaways from this clear dichotomy. For one, I don't think that one motivation was better than the other. However, I think it is important to note that once they knew what they were doing this whole college thing for, it was a lot easier to tailor their Georgetown experience towards that set goal because clear goal setting is one of the ways that you can sort of elevate yourself into premier academic excellency. The point is possessing the ability of being able to recognize what your goal is and tailoring your actions accordingly.

The consistent thing is at least they knew what they wanted and therefore they were able to navigate the Georgetown culture in the way that they wanted to. It also seems as though that both of them have had mainly extrinsic motivation guiding their paths at Georgetown.

I also had the opportunity to interview Betsy Corcoran, Georgetown alumna and the founder and CEO of an EdTech company, EdSurge. Betsy was tremendously insightful in my research as it seemed as though she was mainly guided by learning for learning's sake.

Unlike John or Edgar, she was not sure what the next steps looked like after graduation. However, she was a strong proponent of practicing mindfulness. This was demonstrated by her enrolling into classes in order to learn for learning's sake, even if the class was going to be a clear challenge for her (as evidenced by her degree in economics and mathematics).

Overall, Betsy definitely enjoyed doing what she was doing and she took the classes for what they were and really tried to learn from them. In other words, she ensured she did as many readings as she could, digging deeper to understand the "why" behind certain concepts and formulas, and worked closely with her professors.

I think that's an important distinction between her and the

other two because there are ways to do well in classes without necessarily internalizing the information that you're getting. When learning for learning's sake, you shift from merely memorizing the information and giving the professor what they want to truly understanding all facets of the presented information.

Once you touch down on campus, you have the autonomy and free reign to seek after anything you want. Although you may not understand what it is right away, at least be open to exploring what the possibilities could be and how your time in college could be the means to a possible end. However, ensure that your time in college is because you want to be there as opposed to feeling coerced into it. If coercion is your reasoning for matriculating, you are most likely finished before you even get started.

KEY TAKEAWAYS

- College is a huge investment; know why you're pursuing the degree!
- Although it's important to acknowledge how 3rd parties can influence your purpose, make sure your final rationale for "why" is determined by you and not these 3rd parties.
- Understanding your purpose allows you to augment your college experience to exactly what you want it to be as opposed

to blindly navigating while hoping for the best; everything should be purposeful.

- There is no such thing as a "good" purpose or a "bad" purpose; you just need to have a purpose or, at the very least, are spending time trying to discover that purpose!

PART 2

REFINING YOUR STRATEGY AND DEVELOPING YOUR COMPETITIVE ADVANTAGE

CHAPTER 4

EXTRACURRICULAR INVOLVEMENT

———

WHAT YOU'LL LEARN:

- The dangers of overcommitting yourself.
- My proposed methodology for balancing extracurriculars for both students that have work-study jobs and students that don't have them.

Undoubtedly, Georgetown's campus involvement is thriving as a result of the numerous student-led organizations that the university offers. If you can conceive it, chances are there's a club for it!

In order to promote freshman involvement within said clubs,

it offers a student activity fair at the beginning of each semester. This typically takes place on the front lawn and gives student organizations the opportunity to pitch the mission and vision of their respective clubs to wide-eyed and eager freshmen.

So. Many. Clubs.

I couldn't decide what I wanted to do! Did I want to write for "The Hoya", rise through the ranks, and become a premier writer on campus, reminiscent of President Barack Obama? Or better yet, did I want to get involved with the student government in order to become president of the student body and recreate the success of President Bill Clinton, who attended Georgetown and became president of the student body?

So. Many. Choices.

I had no idea what direction I wanted to go and where I ultimately wanted to end up at.

So I did what any rational, eager freshman would do.

I signed up for everything.

* * *

A.T.TIME.E.N.D.

I quickly realized that I made a mistake. After that fair, my schedule was getting booked like crazy for the various meetings that I signed myself up for. Although it was a great learning experience to discover the numerous opportunities available at Georgetown in retrospect, I almost fell into the trap of overcommitting myself to a variety of organizations.

After feeling overwhelmed, I performed a cost-benefit analysis for the different clubs that I had signed up for. After successful analysis, I was able to dwindle my list down to the 2 clubs that I was most passionate about (based on their missions and the type of people that were present at the meetings I went to). Without a doubt, my due diligence evidenced here was a defining moment, in terms of my positive academic trajectory.

I truly believe that extracurricular involvement should be at 2 organizations, 3 max.

In addition, in your first semester of college, I think one should consider not even joining any organizations that require you to fill an extensive role. The focus should truly remain on your gaining comfortability with the campus and proper campus acclimation was these are frameworks that lend themselves to academic success.

Don't give the campus too much of yourself; at least, not yet.

NEGATIVE IMPACTS OF
OVERCOMMITTING YOURSELF

In high school, I was the type of student to take the hardest classes available to me while also stretching myself thin by being involved with a lot of organizations. Some of my extracurricular involvements included being the captain of the varsity football team, being a mentor through special programs, routinely going to the gym, and being a member of the principal's leadership team. Therefore, each year, I would find myself getting to school around 6am to get my lift in for football season and would not leave school until 6pm. This 6pm leave time would happen year round as either I was in season for football or I had numerous club and activity meetings after school to tend to.

As you might have guessed, this took a toll on my physical well-being, especially considering I was taking the hardest classes available to me (an ill-advised combination of honors and AP classes with 1 easy elective if I was lucky). I found myself showering once I got home, taking a nap, eating, then doing my homework with the hopes of being in the bed to sleep by 11pm. For 3 and 1/4 years of my life, this was my routine for every week day during the school year.

Honestly, it sucked.

In retrospect, my over commitment to some of these organizations was simply due to me being ushered into these roles as opposed to me having a genuine passion or interest.

As I was gearing up for the start of my undergraduate career, I vowed to put myself first when beginning to traverse the campus terrain and figure out what I wanted to be involved in. As you can see with the aforementioned anecdote, it didn't exactly play out that way initially.

After multiple sign ups, I attended a lot of meetings. And I mean a lot of meetings. But in the first two weeks, I started going to less and less meetings and ended up only being a part of 2 clubs that semester. Without a doubt, it was one of the best decisions of my life. Not only did I have enough "free" time in order to comfortably get acclimated to Georgetown's campus climate, I also had enough time to get enough sleep at night and socialize with my friends, all aspects I deem as imperative to building a solid foundation for your collegiate career upon. The result of this approach resulted in me receiving the best grades of my undergraduate career (that wouldn't be eclipsed until Fall 2016).

Some of my other peers have not been as lucky as me, unfortunately. I interviewed a junior at Georgetown named Mia, who is pre-med. During her time at Georgetown, she has been involved with numerous organizations ranging from grassroots organizing, pre-med clubs, work study jobs, a sorority, and everything in between. This trend started in the first semester of her freshman year and has been spiraling ever since.

Admittedly so, she is not naturally adept in the pre-med classes. Therefore, she concedes that she needs to spend a lot of time studying in order to do well in her classes so that she can ultimately fulfill her dream of becoming a doctor. However, she does not study as much as she should be. The reason why?

She has a hard time saying no to people while taking on a lot of responsibility.

Due to her kind nature, she always strives to be there for people and help them if they are ever in trouble. As you could probably expect, when it comes to logistics in running an organization, there are many inevitable challenges that are sure to cause things to go awry. When these things happened, Mia was always there. Sometimes she would volunteer herself to clean up the broken parts. Other times she was called upon. In each time, however, she rose to the occasion.

Mia's talents were not just reserved for when things were going wrong in an organization either. As a result of her passion and interest for a wide variety of different things, she would actively seek different positions and leadership roles that helped her get further exposure in their fields. Although many of her friends and loved ones considered her participation in a high volume of activities ill advised, she continued her pursuit anyway, despite the impact it was having on her academic performance.

At this point in her college career, she is happy with what she has done on campus and the potential legacy that she might leave. However, she acknowledges the fact that giving so much of herself to Georgetown activities may have very significant ramifications when it comes to her pursuit of becoming a doctor.

Let's switch it up and provide an example of someone involved in a high volume of extracurriculars that is doing well academically.

I interviewed another junior at Georgetown named Lauren. She has enjoyed a high level of academic performance during her undergraduate collegiate experience in addition to obtaining several accolades. To the naked eye, Lauren is living the dream. Not only is she enjoying outstanding grades, but she is also involved with many on campus activities and has several campus leadership roles. By all statistical measures, she is the model student.

However, if you catch Lauren on a day-to-day basis, you get a different perspective. Since she is involved with so many activities, in addition to taking a full course-load, she is constantly on the go. Her schedule is usually jam-packed between class, meetings, and getting to her school-work at the very end of the day. When it comes to time management, Lauren is pretty diligent about trying to complete things for her activities in a timely fashion, although she is not always successful.

When it comes to her academics, however, she tends to procrastinate until the very last moment. When it comes to exams and assessments, she tends to wait until the night before , or the day of in some cases, as she will cram. The crazy thing about her approach is that although she acknowledges this form of preparation is not the most effective or reliable method, she continues to adopt it as it is the only method that is fully compatible with her hectic, jam-packed schedule.

This behavior is not new, however. In fact, she is falling into some of the same cycles that she fell into in high school.

Similarly to me, Lauren was highly involved in her public high school while also taking the hardest courses available. Without a doubt, she was *the* school leader that everyone went to whether it came to get her thoughts on the implementation on a new campus policy, how the student government could do more for its students while still operating within the confines of their power, and even how to take their cheerleading to the next level (as she was a cheerleader). She would find herself not returning home until well after the sun went down while also finding herself arriving at school before the sunrise; it was a hard-knock life indeed.

Unfortunately, this lifestyle definitely took its toll on her throughout school. At one point, the stress and exhaustion became so much that she had a break down and found herself crying profusely. Thankfully, her support system was strong enough to lift her spirits while also being able to help her get through the year. However, the fact is that although she was able to make it through high school and be accepted into some of the top institutions, including the ivy league, her hard earned success did come with a price. Although she is doing very well academically at Georgetown, at what cost is this coming?

Do the ends really justify the means?

FINDING THE RIGHT BALANCE

"Students who hold full- or part-time jobs while attending school may engage more in time management behaviors to handle their busy schedules and perform well in their pursuits." (https://www.researchgate.net/publication/209836182_College_Students'_Time_Management_Correlations_With_Academic_Performance_and_Stress)

According to a study conducted by Ekiti State, "The results revealed that procrastination, prioritization and planning were strong indices that affected the students' academic performance in relation to time management. It was strongly recommended that students have to be conscious of time in performing their academic activities so that the level of their academic performance can be high."

In a study conducted in Kazakhstan, the findings showed, "According to the survey results, students with high GPA are likely to have outstanding time management skills. Therefore, those students devote much time to academic related activities outside the class (reading books, working on projects, completing assignments). As respondents stated, it is urgent to manage time effectively in order to succeed in study and participate in the social life of school." (more can be found here: http://yun.moluch.ru/archive/5/296/)

You've seen the research. Now let's see what the A.T.T.E.N.D. method recommends. The proposed methodologies are designed for both students who take on work-study jobs and for students who don't.

I've also set the average hours of work a week for a work-study job to be 10-15 hours as I've found in my research that this tends to be the ideal range for students.

This methodology is also assuming you are taking the average amount of credit hours for *your* school. For some context, Georgetown's average is 15 credit hours while Duke's average is 12 credit hours. Although university averages are different, I would still recommend the following methodology to be tested with your school's average credit hours.

1. Extracurriculars *without* a job/internship set at 10-15 hours a week
    a. If choosing to focus on 1 organization, you can allocate up to as much time as you want, theoretically. You probably won't exceed more than 8 hours (and that's pushing it).
        - You can choose to take on a primary leadership role, such as president.
    b. If choosing to focus on 2 organizations, you can allocate up to 4 hours, on average, per week to each organization.
        - In the first organization, you can choose to assume a primary leadership role (president). In the second organization, you can choose to assume a secondary leadership role (such as vice president or treasurer); you should have enough time to do both.
    c. If choosing to focus on 3 organizations, you can allocate up to 3 hours, on average, per week to each organization.
        - In this methodology, do not pursue leadership roles in all 3 organizations. In the first organization, you can choose to assume a primary leadership role (president). In the 2nd organization, you can also choose to assume

a secondary leadership position (such as vice president or treasurer). In the 3rd organization, be a general body member and do not assume primary, secondary, or tertiary leadership roles.

    d.   Do not exceed 3 organizations.

- Time breakdown for job/internship and extracurriculars per week: A= 5+ hours; B= 8 hours; C= 9 hours

2.   Extracurriculars *with* a job/internship set at 10-15 hours a week

    a.   If choosing to focus on 1 organization, you can allocate up to an average of 4 hours.

        ▪ You can choose to assume a primary or secondary leadership position (such as president/vice president/treasurer) .

    b.   If choosing to focus on 2 organizations, you can allocate up to an average of 3 hours to the most important organization and up to an average of 2 hours to the secondary organization.

        ▪ You can choose either a primary or secondary leadership position (such as president/vice president/treasurer) primary organization. Assume a secondary leadership position for the secondary organization (with consideration of being a general body member dependent on the rigor of the primary organization).

    c.   If choosing to focus on 3 organizations, you can allocate up to an average of 2 hours for the primary organization, an average of 2 hours for the secondary organization, and an average of 1 hour for the tertiary organization.

- You can assume a secondary leadership role (such as vice president or treasurer). In your secondary organization, you can assume a secondary leadership role (such as treasurer) or being a general body member. In your tertiary organization, I only recommend you being a general body member.

   d.   Do not exceed 3 organizations.

- Time breakdown for job/internship and extracurriculars per week: A= 14-18 hours; B= 15-20 hours; C= 15-20 hours

POINT OF CLARIFICATION

As you might notice, working or pursuing an internship forces you to dedicate more hours in your week to something. Do not be intimidated by this. Just because the absence of a job or internship gives you more time to complete school work does not necessarily mean you will. We will explore this concept further in Chapter 6.

CHAPTER 5

TIME MANAGEMENT

WHAT YOU'LL LEARN:

- The importance of time management and how research suggests this is imperative to academic success.
- Different methods that can help you manage your time for effectively

"Bruh, Calculus is literally the Bain of my existence right now. I literally don't understand implicit differentiation and the test is on Tuesday. I've been so stressed out by this test that I've only slept 4 hours in the past 2 days." -Aaron

"Man, I feel you. This MacroEcon test has got me stressing. I just don't get it, I've never missed a class, do all the homework, attend office hours AND recitation, yet I still don't get this!

It's just...*sniffles* it just sucks when you try your best but your best just isn't good enough you know?" Kyle said while trying not to cry.

My chuckling across the table instantly makes their eyes verge towards my direction

"And what the hell are you laughing at?!" -Aaron

With one headphone in my ear, "This episode of Malcolm in the Middle has me WEAK bro! Malcolm just got grounded but said it was all worth it and then sniffed a girl's bra! Classic!"

An eerie silence came over the table

"...Why, what's up?" I responded, completely oblivious to the aforementioned conversation.

"Nothing, except for the fact that I haven't slept in days and that Kyle is on the verge of an emotional breakdown!"- Aaron

"Damn... that's wild. I'd suggest the both of you take a nap."

"Nap?! You have some audacity to suggest something so friv-olous! WE DON'T HAVE TIME TO SLEEP!" -Aaron

"For one, lower your voice; I don't know who you think you're talking to like that. Secondly, I'm taking both of the same midterms as you and Kyle and I took a nap today... on top of getting 8 hours of sleep last night. So... somebody's lying."

"Well we all can't be privileged like you!"

Considering I was on the verge of homelessness and have had bouts with poverty all throughout my life, I never really considered myself privileged. I was just trying to "spread the gospel," essentially, and let them know why I rarely appeared to be stressed; I had adept time management skills, took naps, and got enough sleep at night.

After further conversation, both of them concluded that my advice was ill-advised and were sure that their lack of sleep and constant state of perpetual anxiety would result in better grades on the respective midterms. Let's check the stats:

CALCULUS MIDTERM 1

Adrian: 92%

Aaron: 79%

MACROECON MIDTERM 1

Adrian: 25/30 (above the curve's median)

Kyle: 21/30 (below the curve's median)

I don't like to be the friend that says "I told you so" but… I sent them Snapchats of me snuggled in my bed, as if I was about to take a nap, with the caption as: "Spreading the gospel."

They were pissed.

* * *

A.T.TIME.E.N.D.

When you are embarking on a collegiate journey, I think it is very important to have the understanding that although you have more time in college than you did in high school, it will really seem that time is consistently scarce in comparison to your high school days. I really can't pinpoint why that is but there seems to be a general consensus amongst my peers about why this occurs including an increase in academic rigor, being involved with numerous organizations, or trying to obtain and ultimately balance different internships. And don't even get me started on trying to effectively manage your social life.

As you can see, there are so many different worlds that will ultimately encompass your collegiate experience and being able to effectively navigate all of these worlds can only be made possible through time management. For most college students, you will want to be able to perform at a high level in all of these different spheres. In order to do so, you need to make sure that each sphere has proper time allocation.

When trying to decide where your time should be spent, I would highly encourage you to start with your academics.

Generally speaking based on different feedback that I've gotten from professors and different research that I've done in addition to talking with different students, they would recommend that, at least early on in your collegiate experience in your undergraduate career, you should definitely do your work well in advance because it gives you optimum time.

For one, it allows you to go back over your work which means you are essentially going over it twice to make sure the what you did the first time was correct.

Secondly, it gives you time to get feedback from your professor or to get feedback from a peer that is better in the class than you and so on and so forth.

Lastly, it is nice not having to worry about things at the last minute because procrastination really is a big issue for college students and I'm sure it is even an issue for high school students. I know it was for me but in high school but the key difference was that I was able to procrastinate and still get A's.

In college, if I procrastinate, I am putting myself into murky territory and severely risking my overall grade as things are graded much more intensely in college.

This is not to say that everyone that procrastinates won't get good grades (because you will definitely find kids in college that can, even though I am willing to argue they are few and far in between) but in order to achieve the optimum level of of happiness and still enjoy being in comfort, one must get their habit of procrastinating under control.

Allow me to illustrate this point.

Let's say you're procrastinating and you're trying to finish an assignment for the morning by pulling an all nighter. You are most likely stressed, tired, and dreading your undergraduate experience at that given moment. Juxtapose this feeling to if you did this assignment days in advance. You would be cruising into the last night thinking that, "I've already done what I've done in advance and this is pretty good since I've gotten recommendations and feedback from my professor. Not to mention, I even had a friend look over it! I'll probably only spend like maybe 20 minutes on this tonight in order to tie up any loose ends." The immediate after math of this approach includes getting a good night's sleep and a place of serenity. The long-term benefit?

Euphoria.

$$* * *$$

This chapter was inspired a lot by my interview with Jeffrey, also a student at Georgetown doing extremely well academically, because he was saying that a lot of his friends don't believe that you can have a great social life, get enough sleep and still have stellar academics. In his opinion, he is the complete antithesis to this notion since he is the living, breathing example of being able to do all of those different things because he allocates enough time.

Another key aspect he noted as beneficial was having the ability to handle ad-hoc crisis situations. This only came as the result of his impeccable time management skills. As college students, you will be thrusted into an environment where everyone is coming from a different background and dealing with a wide variety of different factors. As a result, you might encounter serious crisis situations whether you are the one experiencing them or you are hearing this the situation second hand from a friend. What is even worse is that these situations can occur when you are still expected to perform in the variety of other spheres you encompass; life does not stop.

Therefore, Jeffrey argued that being able to have time allocated in his schedule as genuine "free-time" was immensely beneficial as he will, in theory, have time to handle his own problems or act as a support system for when his friends are facing trials and tribulations. All the while, he still has the space be there while not detracting from the other spheres of his life. This is not a case of "either/or"; rather, it is about "and/both."

Let me provide another example.

John graduated a couple of years ago and for much of his freshman and sophomore year, he very much had a Jeffrey approach where he was ensuring that he was getting his assignments done four to five to six days in advance because he was diligent about ensuring that he had enough time to do so. As he got older, particularly in his junior and senior year, he began to develop a stronger understanding of his strengths and decided to tweak his routine methodology.

For example, as I mentioned earlier, in his freshman and sophomore year, he would make sure that he would get his papers done well in advance but in his junior and senior year, he said he started doing his papers the night before because he knew that he could still get A's even with such short notice. That is why I would recommend being more efficient in the early stages of your college career simply because you don't have enough time to understand how you're going to to do when pitted against collegiate academics.

Therefore, I would encourage you to err on the side of caution in your first couple of years at the very least. After that, if you actually have a better understanding, as far as what your professors are asking of you and knowing that you can still be effective, in terms of putting out a damn good product, then maybe you can alter your methodology and complete work the night before or two days before as opposed to the 3 or 4 or 5 days that you were doing your freshman year and sophomore years.

I firmly believe that as you get older, you become wiser in the sense of knowing for a fact what you can and cannot do the night before and still getting an A. That's not something that most people know, at least in their first year in college, because they are immersed in a completely different environment. However, after getting accustomed to said environment, that is when you can start making those game-time decisions that entail understanding the quality of product that you want to put out in a lesser amount of time.

"What if I'm a procrastinator by nature?"

I've had interviews with people that are procrastinators that ended up stopping. Their reasoning for why they were able to stop being procrastinators simply came from the the internal shift that happened. Literally, it was just like one day they realized they did not want to live that lifestyle anymore that entailed rushing to finish their schoolwork. It was at that moment they made the lifestyle change to start getting their homework done in advance and stuck to it.

Although you will most likely have many people constantly telling you to "get your work done in advance; get your work in advance; get your work done in advance." it only becomes apparent when you're ready to do it for yourself.

It is unfortunate but if I was able to break that wall and figure out exactly what it takes to get someone to do something besides just telling them or besides them just recognizing that they want to do it for themselves, I think I'd be a rich man to be honest. Until that day comes, "I can lead a horse to water but I can't make them drink it."

I also ended up interviewing one of my peers named Shakera. She is currently a sophomore at Georgetown and went from not making the Dean's List in her first semester to making the Dean's list in her second semester in college. What is unique and compelling about her is that she was a classic procrastinator in high school that was able to get away with doing her work at the very last minute and tried to apply that same methodology in college. After she realized her grades were not where she wanted them to be, she decided to make a change; one of these changes included doing her schoolwork in a timely fashion.

In her current state, she is on the upturn of being able to be less of a procrastinator but as she reflected on her collegiate experiences during the interview, she talked about in the past that she would usually be up late at night doing homework at the last minute. In her fall semester of freshman year, it got to the point that her doing homework late at night was not only affecting her output, but it was also resulting in her getting less sleep that also contributed to her not getting good grades.

So in her second semester, she decided to make her academics a priority. This meant going in to her professors' office hours more, getting her work done well in advance, etc. Although she concedes that she is not where she wants to be in terms of the aforementioned skills she is trying to attain, she was an example of someone striving for these proper time efficient methodologies directly improving her academic performance.

Although I have talked a lot about advanced preparation increasing your academic performance, I know for a fact that during your undergraduate experience, you will run into students that can get good grades even while procrastinating. However, in most cases, it was not the most viable option, in terms of their overall happiness and in terms of their overall well-being. Although you can still be good at school, meaning that you obtain good grades, while procrastinating, I would challenge you to understand that you can be good at school, not procrastinate, and have an overall better sense of your well-being.

* * *

All in all, I think it just comes down to really prioritizing your homework and really prioritizing academics. Let's keep in mind what Jeffrey says: if you do want to do well and if you do want to be academically elite, this has to be a top priority whether you like it or not (unless you are super genius; if you're a super genius, you're probably not reading this book. So using logical deductive reasoning, we can conclude that you are not a super genius).

THE METHOD

- Create a calendar whether digitally (on your cell phone, computer, tablet, etc.) or traditionally (in your notebook or planner). Record everything, if possible.
  - ◆ Ensure deadlines are clearly marked in your calendar not only the day of, but 3 days our from when they are due.
- Ensure that you incorporate 7-8 hours of sleep a night into your schedule
  - ◆ This is a non-negotiable. Therefore, you must decide how extracurriculars, class schedules, etc. will work around this.
    - ▪ If you absolutely *have* to take an 8am (avoid at all cost!), that would mean your bed time needs to be 11:30pm-12:30am with a 7:30am wake up time.

- Ensure that you are completing your most important tasks first.
- Dedicate time to the things that help you decompress and relieve stress such as exercising and catching up on your favorite shows.
- End your day at a fixed time—no exception. If you truly believe in your fixed time to complete all of your tasks in a given day, you will be forcing yourself to complete your tasks against this time; this psychological shift will be working in your subconscious.

POINT OF CLARIFICATION

In my opinion, you can still have adept time management skills while still having a vibrant social life. However, I do not definite a vibrant social life as one of those things where you are constantly drunk every single weekend. If that's your perception of what a great social life looks like, that's fine, but I would also challenge your understanding of why you're at college. Furthermore, I would challenge you to put these two ideologies at the table.

You may talk about you wanting to have like a stellar social life that entails partying every weekend (whether it is midterm week or finals week) but let's really think about it—why did you want to come to college in the first place? Secondly, do you want to do well academically here? If you don't want to do well academically this is the wrong book for you (so you might have just wasted your money buying this book...unless you are reading a free pdf, in which case all I have to say is you won this round).

In a last ditch attempt to allow you to see it from my perspective, I would encourage you to perform some cost-benefit analysis to each approach. So if you're one of those students that you are prioritizing your social life, characterized by partying, over your academics, let us less look at the positives and negatives.

Positives: a lot of memorable nights, probably more hook ups, and always having something to do on the weekends.

Negatives: less time to study, not always getting the chance to get to know people outside of a party setting, higher chances of getting into trouble, and probably getting worse grades.

In my opinion, although I only listed one more negative than positive, I would argue that the negatives carry far more weight than the positives. By that, I am suggesting that while the positives provide short term gratification, the negatives provide long-term ramifications that can potentially detrimental for your future endeavors and whatever you are striving for.

Although I'm sure that I can come up with even more negatives (and you can too), the fact remains that if you're prioritizing your academics over your social life, that does not mean you are inevitably subjugated to be a hermit either. It just means that in your eyes, your academics are first and foremost while striving to find that healthy dose of social life for you. This approach has worked wonders for several of the individuals that I have interviewed including Jeffrey, John, and even myself.

CHAPTER 6

EFFICIENCY

WHAT YOU'LL LEARN

- How I came to discovering the importance of efficiency.
- Research suggesting the importance of efficiency.
- A step by step plan of how to increase efficiency in your schedule.

By the time sophomore year rolled around, I felt as though I had a pretty good handle on Georgetown. I wasn't overcommitting myself to clubs, was figuring out how I needed to prep for each class, and had a vibrant social life. I felt good about where I was at!

However, I was only working 6 hours a week and after my freshman year, I quickly realized that this work week setup wasn't sustainable. I needed some spending money to keep the burden off my family and that meant finding a way to make cash without cutting into my grades. One of the things I'd seen others struggle with is balancing the two: oftentimes choosing too many hours at a minimum wage job at the expense of your grades. Naturally, I sought after an increase in my work hours but hoping not see my grades suffer.

Sometimes you've got to be careful with what you ask for.

In order for me to get the increase in work hours, it required me to take on a leadership position. I thought this leadership position would bring my total work hours to 12 in a given week.

Nope.

16-20 hours. That was the amount of time I was supposed to dedicate to my job every week including being on call in some cases.

Even though I could feasibly fit this new addition into my schedule, it made things that much tighter.

These circumstances led me to learning one of my greatest collegiate lessons: the importance of efficiency.

* * *

A.T.T.EFFICIENCY.N.D.

In this semester, I learned that even though college gives one more free time and flexibility, in comparison to high school, it's actually quite deceitful. I aptly dub this realization as "pseudo free-time."

* * *

Cyril Northcote Parkinson made a groundbreaking statement when he wrote, "Work expands to fill the time available for its completion."; this has been dubbed as "Parkinson's Law." Many industry leader's success has been predicated on this creed; let's unpack it.

Essentially, as a rule of thumb, Parkinson argued that work/tasks only took as long to complete as the time you've allotted for it. Still confused? I'll provide an example.

Let's say you have an assignment to complete. You look at it and you estimate you'll need 4 hours to complete the assignment. It's due one week from today. What most people in college do is say, "Great, I have a week to complete it... I'll do it whenever I have time to complete it and maybe will spend some *extra* time on it since I have week."

Using Parkinson's Law, most college students will take the entire week to complete it... and for most college students knowing the deadline is a week from today, we'll finish it in the four to six-hour period before it's due. We didn't spend any more than the four hours of time it required — except for some of the stress we had thinking maybe we'd do it early, maybe we'd start pieces of it, etc.

Here's the problem: it took you 4 hours of to complete, you added unnecessary stress to your life, AND you still probably finished the assignment at the end right before it's due. This, I'd argue, is highly inefficient.

But let's reimagine how we could use Parkinson's Law to our advantage:

Take the same scenario — you've got an assignment that you estimate will take four hours that's due in a week. Instead of saying you'll do it "this week" go ahead and schedule a four-hour block of time whenever you plan to complete it (ideally at least 2 days before). Budget no more time than those four hours and do it in a study block of time you've set aside. Then stop thinking about it entirely.

When the block of time comes along, you've set aside four hours to complete it. Use the four hours to complete it and be done at that time. Because you set aside 4 hours for completion, according to the law, you will most likely complete it in said 4 hours. In retrospect, you may realize you could have completed the assignment in 3 hours instead of 4. This is also an important realization to have as continued refinement and practice of the law will allow you to make efficient guestimations of time needing to be required.

Yes, Parkinson's Law really can cut both ways: if you aren't being efficient with your time you'll spend all your time completing tasks; but if you are efficient you'll only allocate the specific time you estimated for the assignment or project. And for me, that was the key to actually starting to work efficiently: not letting the time between assignments drive how much time I spent on it vs. letting the time I estimated on the assignment drive the time I spent.

If you have four hours to complete an assignment and that's the block you've set aside, then that's what you'll fill. But if you set aside "a week" then your brain will, in many ways, convince you that you *should* be working on the assignment whenever you're not.

And that's why Parkinson's Law can become a college student's very best (or worst) friend. Thank you, Cyril.

* * *

With the addition of a new role at work, my established time management skills would be tested in ways in which they had never been tested before.

In my first week of this new job, I quickly found myself falling behind on work. Rapidly, it was as if an avalanche comprised of tedious homework, pop quizzes, group projects, and term papers was honing in on me.

What was so different about last year than this semester? Whilst in this process of self-reflection, I learned that I was allotted more time for my homework while having more time to spend engaging in frivolous things such as watching movies or playing video games.

In the previous semesters, I would save most of my homework for the night. At night, I could give myself hours upon hours to do my homework at whatever pace I deemed acceptable. Admittedly, my pace was abysmal. When writing papers, for example, I would complete a paragraph or two, gain an unwarranted sense of accomplishment, then glide over to Youtube and become lost in the world of "related videos."

While I recognize that it was unproductive, it didn't really matter because I still completed my work in a timely fashion, in advance, before everything was due. Now that time was literally of the essence, things had to change fast.

I reached out to several mentors who appeared to be busier

than I but seemed to have a knack for appearing calm under what I would deem as stressful situation. In their advice, they helped me shift my paradigm of understanding of time.

* * *

Even though you should have proper time allocations already incorporated into your schedule, efficiency becomes the key to getting the most out of your time. If you're giving yourself a two-hour block for your homework, you need to make sure that you're actually completing your homework in that block of time and ensure that you're not goofing off on YouTube or that you're not surrounding yourself with individuals that taking away from the work that you're doing.

Therefore, I think efficiency is a part of the one-two punch, essentially, where you must first put yourself in a position to succeed; first punch. The second punch is understanding that efficiency is ensuring that you are completing your work at a very high level while maintaining strong pacing and, at times, trying to be under the time that you allocated for yourself.

In turn, this fits into the overall grand scheme and notion of being able to set aside enough time and still being to handle all of your obligations including extracurricular, homework, and getting a great night's rest.

If you're able to be even more efficient than what you originally planned and allocated for yourself, you have time to do whatever the hell you want to do, essentially. I love having time just to just mess around and, to be honest, messing around without the fear of collegiate obligations looming over me is one of my favorite parts about college.

Being efficient and even working faster than the efficiency that you have sort of created for yourself just leads to more time to do whatever you want to do whether that's to mess around and be unproductive, to start your own entrepreneurial endeavor, or to just do whatever makes you happy, essentially.

At this point, you might be asking yourself, what does efficiency actually look like?

Efficiency comes down to actually getting your work done at a high level in a timely fashion with minimal breaks, plain and simple.

While we are on the topic of breaks, although I believe you can definitely incorporate different sorts of breaks into your study period, you need to be vigilant about how much work is actually getting done.

Therefore, in order to better illustrate my point, I will provide an example of inefficiency. In the beginning of my freshman year, I would be in the library writing my paper and after typing a couple sentences for my essay, I would feel an undue sense of accomplishment and then go on Instagram and find myself lost on the "explore" page for 15-30 minutes. After snapping back into reality, I would realize I am still behind on my paper and then get back to my essay.

Let's break this situation down.

In this instance, it could be argued that I am demonstrating versatility in the sense of being able to multi-task. Although this is a skill that I believe my generation is better at than others, I do not believe this should be incorporated when studying or doing homework unless in extreme circumstances (and most of the time, there are not many circumstances like that). Therefore, when your grades are on the line, I believe you should keep those two spheres separate.

When deciding to either do your work or take a break, ensure that you are doing one or the other without overlap. If I'm typing my paper, I would most likely give myself a time limit (1 to 2 hours in a given sitting) In this sitting, I am incorporating my different citations, I am ensuring that my points are all arguing in favor of my thesis, and overall, I am giving the paper its due diligence.

If I am taking a break, I need to be taking a break to the fullest extent. Therefore, I am catching up on social media, I am listening to my favorite podcasts, and I am just enjoying my momentary break without the state of perpetual fear of me neglecting my work (with proper time limits on said break).

I have found, and I am sure you will find as well, that my best breaks come from me not worrying about any responsibilities at that given moment. In order to achieve this feeling, not only do I have to be efficient enough to put myself in that position, but I must also exude an element of mindfulness at that current moment in order to ensure that I am getting the most out of that break.

* * *

With the help of several mentors, I was able to understand that they tended to do more with less. In this case, having less time, in most cases, did not affect their overall product output. In fact, after recognizing they had less time, they made their necessary adjustments and then developed a strategic plan of attack. In fact, the key nuance in their plan of attack was an increase of overall efficiency. Essentially, whether it was school work, regular work, going to the cafeteria, etc., they ensured they were completing these tasks without getting distracted by external factors.

Ah-ha! That was it. I needed to develop my own plan of attack and gain a stronger sense of focus; if I didn't have tunnel-vision at this point, I'd have to develop it quickly.

In order to develop a plan that was effective, I had to ensure it was comprised of comprehensive understanding of my daily schedule.

So that's what I did. I decided to continue my regular routine for Monday through Wednesday (the busiest days of the week for me that didn't include my work study job since that was a non-negotiable) and document how much time I was spending for my biggest activities. I determined that the biggest factors in my schedule were eating at the dining hall, socializing with my friends, and doing homework.

A simple trip to the dining hall ended up being a two-hour endeavor as a result of me seeing other friends and just shooting the breeze with them. To make matters worse, a large part of my meal was spent socializing even though this wasn't my designated time for it.

Socializing tended to range anywhere from an hour and a half to three hours. Don't get me wrong, the results of these conversations were always fascinating and I'm happy to have had them, but at the same time, the amount of time that I was dedicating to those conversations would have been better spent in trying to complete my homework; academics were taking a backseat to my friends and I believe that order needs to be reversed and should only be broken amidst extenuating circumstances.

Lastly, the time I designated for homework was one to four hours. However, just because I spent more time on homework did not equate to me getting more work done. When I gave myself longer blocks (i.e. four hours), I found myself getting the same amount of work done (sometimes less) than when I gave myself 1 hour blocks.

Longer times allotted for homework does *not always* equate to more homework getting done.

After analyzing the aforementioned realizations, I began to make the necessary modifications to my schedule. First, it started with my time at the dining hall. Instead of meandering there until God knows when, I decided to give myself a 30-minute cap if I was going to eat pre-prepared food or 45 minutes if I was going to eat food that was made on the spot. I still socialized and what not during my meal, but the time cap forced me to be conscious of how long I was eating my food and having the self-discipline to leave once my time was up.

Next, I restructured the time I was spending with my friends. Because I genuinely valued the conversations and the time we were spending, I was very hesitant when it came to reducing my time with them.

So I didn't.

Instead, I chose to get my work done first before hanging out with them. One of the things I discovered was that when I hung out with my friends before doing my homework, I would find myself worried about the impending assignments lurking. I was not as invested in the conversation simply do to a constant state of worry.

Once I reversed the order, I found myself more engaged in the conversations as I didn't have to worry about what still needed to be done for the day. My only worry was ensuring that I didn't stay up too late so that I could still go to bed and get 8 hours of sleep.

Lastly, when it came to homework, I decided to change up my entire attack. Instead of waiting to the night to be productive, I found that mid-day work sessions were even better. The pockets of free time that you might have in between classes (30 minutes to 2 hours) can and should be utilized in order to ensure you are academically successful.

In addition, since these times were set (meaning that I had something before and after those windows of time), I forced myself to be engaged with what I was doing. Pragmatically, I turned off my phone (not really—just put it on Do Not Disturb!), closed Facebook, Youtube, etc. from my internet browser, and got to work. I didn't deviate from the task at hand and, sure enough, I found my level of efficiency increasing tenfold as a result.

* * *

THE PLAN

Step 1: Reflect on your week and determine what your 3-4 busiest days are according to number of classes, job, and meetings and document how much time is spent in each sector.

Step 2: On the aforementioned busiest days, determine what the rest of your time is consisted of like eating at the dining hall, socializing with your friends, watching Netflix, and designated time for homework and document how much time is spent in each sector.

> **Monday**
> Wake Up: 8:45am
> Class: 9:00am - 10:15am
> Break: 10:15am - 11:00am
> Class: 11:00am - 12:15pm
> Dining Hall: 12:15pm - 2:15pm
> Break: 2:15pm - 3:00pm
> Work-Study: 3:00pm - 6:00pm
> Org Meeting: 6:00pm - 7:30pm
> Dining Hall: 7:30pm - 8:30pm
> Friends: 8:30pm - 10:30pm
> Homework: 10:30pm - Til

Step 3: Examine your findings. The results from your findings in Step 1 are the mainstays in your schedule that cannot be altered (unless you are unhappy and find no value in them; then you may want to consider dropping them). The results from your findings in Step 2 are the arenas in your life that you have most control over. In both cases, you may be surprised by your given time allocations.

Monday

Wake Up : 8:45am
Class : 9:00am - 10:15am
Break : 10:15am - 11:00 am
Class : 11:00am - 12:15pm
Dining Hall : 12:15 pm - 2:15pm
Break : 2:15pm - 3:00pm
Work-Study : 3:00pm - 6:00pm
Org Meeting : 6:00pm - 7:30pm
Dining Hall : 7:30pm - 8:30pm
Friends : 8:30pm - 10:30pm
Homework : 10:30pm - Til

Step 4: Cut your time allocations, in regards to your findings from Step 2. There are 3 categories in which you can choose to cut: A) Cautious (reduce your time allocation in each sector by 1/4th) B) Average (reduce your time allocation in each sector by 1/2) C) Risk-Taker (reduce your time allocation in each sector by 3/4ths).

Although I enjoy calculated risk-taking as much as the next guy, I wouldn't recommend jumping to option C right away. In most cases, option C will not be necessary unless you are spending 2 or 3 hours in EACH arena of Step 2. I chose option B to begin and would recommend starting with option B. It's enough of a push where it will require you to seriously rethink your schedule yet it's not too extreme meaning the margin of error is far more manageable than option C. I would steer away from option A as I feel as though it's not requiring you to get out of your comfort zone enough and leaves you susceptible to revert back to your old ways.

Note: I chopped my time by a 4th for my lunch time dining hall experience. I determined an hour was not necessary for me

Monday Revised

Wake Up : 8:45am
Class 9:00am - 10:15am
Break : 10:15am - 11:00am

Class : 11:00am - 12:15pm
Dining Hall 12:15pm - 12:45pm / 1:00pm
Break 12:45pm / 1:00pm - 3:00pm
Work-Study : 3:00pm - 6:00pm
Org Meeting 6:00pm - 7:30pm
Dining Hall : 7:30pm - 8:00pm / 8:15pm
Friends : 8:30pm - 9:30pm
Homework : 9:30pm - Til

Step 5: Ensure that the new time allocations in your schedule are representative of the "Academics first" philosophy meaning that you will be attempting to get your homework done before dedicated time to socialize with your friends or indulging in your guilty pleasures like Youtube, Netflix, etc.

Work - Study : 3:00pm - 6:00
Org Meeting : 6:00 pm - 7:30 p
Dining Hall : 7:30pm - 8:00pm
Friends : 8:30 pm - 9:30pm
Homework : 9:30pm - Til

Step 6: Reflect on your newly created schedule and see if you have small pockets of free time between things constantly in your schedule. For example, if you have two classes that are 45 minutes apart, dedicate this time to starting some homework, handling emails, completing minute tasks, etc. I changed the name of this time from "Break" to "Productivity" in my schedule.

Monday Revised

Wake Up : 8:45am

Class : 9:00am - 10:15am

Break : 10:15am - 11:00am
Productivity

* Time Saved *

Between 2 hrs 45 mins
and 3hrs

Class : 11:00am - 12:15pm

Dining Hall : 12:15pm - 12:45pm / 1:00pm

Break : 12:45pm / 1:00pm - 3:00pm
Productivity

Work - Study : 3:00pm - 6:00pm

Org Meeting : 6:00pm - 7:30pm

Dining Hall : 7:30pm - 8:00pm / 8:15pm

Friends : 8:30pm - 9:30pm

Homework : 9:30pm - ???

Step 7: STICK TO THE PLAN! The purpose of cutting your time in half is to create a sense of urgency in order to increase your overall level of efficiency. Challenge yourself to complete the tasks at hand within the time you have allotted for yourself. If, and only if, you find yourself completing the tasks within your given timeframes, consider creating a reward system of sorts. Psychological tricks like these are very helpful.

Monday Final

Wake Up: 8.45 am
Class: 9:00 am - 10:15 am
Productivity: 10:15 am - 11:00 am
Class: 11:00 am - 12:15 pm
Dining Hall: 12:15 pm - 12:45 pm / 1:00 pm
Productivity: 12:45 pm / 1:00 pm - 3:00 pm
Work-Study: 3:00 pm - 6:00 pm
Org Meeting: 6:00 pm - 7:30 pm
Dining Hall: 7:30 pm - 8:00 pm / 8:15 pm
Homework: 8:15 pm - 11:45 pm
Friends: 11:45 pm - 12:45 am
Clock-Out: 12:45 am (to get 8 hours of sleep)

Step 8: Adjust as necessary. As you are implementing this plan, please be vigilant about what works and does not work for you. Don't be afraid to adjust this as you need to in order to achieve your desired level of efficiency (and overall success) as this is just a skeletal framework to get you started and is designed to be malleable.

As I found my efficiency increasing, I also found my stress levels proportionally declining. In other words, in my case, there was an inverse relationship between my level of efficiency and my stress levels meaning that if I was less efficient with my time, I would find myself in a perpetual state of worry, thus resulting in stress.

PART 3

WINNING PROFESSORS OVER

CHAPTER 7

WINNING PROFESSORS OVER— CLASS PARTICIPATION

———

WHAT YOU'LL LEARN

- The importance of class participation and how you can leverage these optics in a favorable manner.
- Proposed methodologies for how you can increase your class participation

"Hi Professor S,

Thank you for your response. I will be sure to follow up with her. The reason why I asked is because this was exactly what I was fearing from this class. I was striving for the A and put out what I believed was A work, but did not receive any of the grades throughout the semester to know if I was doing as well as I thought I was doing.

One of my goals was to get an A in the course; at this point, it's highly improbable and it looks like I will have to settle for a B+. I'm going to reflect on my experience within this class this summer and figure out how I can avoid being in this position again. Here's to a lesson learned. Have a great summer!

Best,

Adrian Abrams"

"Hang tight, Adrian. It's not over yet.

Prof. S"

Sure enough, it wasn't over yet. I checked my grade for this class. I couldn't believe it.

"A." Not even an "A-." She turned my "B+" into a flat out "A."

Well I'll be damned.

"Hey Professor S,

You were right, I counted myself out before everything was over. Needless to say, I'm ecstatic! That was the grade I needed to be on Dean's List for the 4th consecutive semester and am elated. Thank you for working with me over the past semester. You provided a lot of wisdom, insight, and it was genuinely nice being able to just talk freely about life. I hope you have a great summer and I *might* see you in the fall in your Intro to Sociology course!

Hoya Saxa,

Adrian Abrams"

"I'm in your corner, Adrian.

:-)

Hoya Saxa"

* * *

A.T.T.E.IN CLASS PARTICIPATION.D.

PROFESSORS

Man, the spring of my sophomore year was tough. Not only was I becoming more entrusted with leadership roles for my chosen organizations, I was also dealing with coursework that was outside of the scope of my natural abilities (in this case, math based courses). As a result, I was having a tougher semester than normal. After being on the Dean's List for the previous 3 semesters, I was worried about the streak terminating.

In one case, the class in the aforementioned story above, I literally did not know what my grade in the class was for the entirety of the semester. To make matters worse, I had three professors. Since I had three professors, I was not really sure who had the most power in the class and who had the final say. Therefore, I had to be strategic in my approach when it came to seeking the best possible grade in this class.

At the beginning of the semester, I knew that office hours and class participation would be imperative to my success in this class especially given the high level of variability when surrounding the grading of assessments. As a result, I chose one of the 3 professors to routinely attend their office hours and made sure to consistently participate in class at it was visible to all 3 of my professors.

In this approach, so many factors played out that ultimately resulted in my professor looking out for me and giving me an A.

CLASS PARTICIPATION

Another great way to win professors over is by participating in class. In terms of the overall optics of the situation, you can easily win some favor over from your professor by showing this form of engagement during class. In most college courses, professors have a hard time getting students to participate. This can be due to the amount of students that can be in a class and how intimidating it might be, students not actually prepping for the class properly, etc. So, once again, this is something that your peers simply aren't doing. As a result, you can create this niche for yourself.

When a professor consistently sees you participating in class, they view you as a valuable contributor to their classroom learning environment. Not only are you asking questions that most students likely have, you are also helping their class go by faster.

Believe it or not, professors feel how grueling a lecture can be just like you do (probably not to the same extent, though, since they are the ones facilitating it).

In addition, participating in class will also increase your academic performance, as research suggests. As mentioned earlier, there are bound to be things that go over your head in class. Instead of being like most students and letting it go, you should make it a point to stop the class and ask a question if anything is unclear to you.

College lectures tend to build on each other. Therefore, if you're missing an essential building block, it will make your construction that much harder. As a result of you clarifying several points in class, you will find that you wont have as hard of a time when completing assignments for the class since you did your due diligence beforehand.

Let's think about it rationally. College is expensive. We know this. Therefore, why would you waste your investment by sitting through college classes and not even understand what's going on? If you are willing to be complacent in that sense, I would argue that you probably should not have gone to class in the first place as it most likely equates to the same thing (unless attendance is mandatory; then that's the only difference).

DIFFERENT APPROACHES

You know that kid in class that always participates whose comments might be spot on or rarely veers from the topic? We all do. What you might not have known is that the kid most likely didn't complete the assigned reading in its entirety for class.

"What's the point of that?"

Well, there are a lot of great benefits that stem from students participating in class.

1) It distinguishes you from other students and allows the professor to recognize you as the student that always participates.

Professors love students that participate, as previously mentioned. Therefore, if you're known as a student that is always *trying* to contribute to class discussions, this won't go unnoticed when professors are giving out final grades. Make no mistake, professors are inherently subjective. Use class participation as a means of gaining leniency for final grade deliberations.

2) Gives you a platform to stand on when advocating for yourself at the end of the semester.

I'm not the type of student to take final grades for face value. In fact, if I receive a grade that I think is either inaccurate, I don't like, or think that I can get bumped up, I go to my professor's office hours to discuss. Whenever I advocate for myself, I always point to class participation as a means of showcasing my effort in class; this point will be expounded upon in the next chapter.

Below you will find tips and tricks for increasing your class participation.

- Set a goal to publicly engage class at least 2 times per week whether it's a thought provoking question or a meaningful comment.

- Do the readings enough to where you can find the central topic and then develop 2 questions or insights to share in class each week; if you're a rockstar and want to contribute more than twice each week, please do. It's better to over-participate than to under-participate.
  - ◆ Ensure that you are creating notes on these points. They are a great reference point for when you need to review material for the class in addition to ensuring you won't forget each point for class.
- Find friends in the class. Create an accountability system where you all have friendly competition to see who can participate the most in class.
- Build off of other points made in class. No need to reinvent the wheel.
- Sit in the front of class. It makes it 10x harder to participate from the back of class.
- Try to make your comments clear and concise and avoid rambling. Your professors will thank you for it.
- Lastly, try to explain what part of the reading your question/comment is being derived from (explicitly cite page number, section, etc.). In terms of optics, it appears as though you actually read (which isn't always the case) and your professor will begin to view you as a hard working student that actually knows what they're talking about.
  - ◆ Again, this doesn't have to necessarily be true, in regards

to always doing your readings, but it's important to create the perception that you do.

Professors can either be your biggest foes or your greatest allies; the choice is yours really. You don't have anything to lose and everything to gain from attending office hours and participating in class.

Do it.

Win them over.

CHAPTER 8

WINNING PROFESSORS OVER–OFFICE HOURS

———

WHAT YOU'LL LEARN

- The importance of office hours and the benefits of attending them routinely.
- Strategies to incorporate when you are attending office hours.

"Hey professor, do you have a moment?"

"Sure, come on in."

"First off, I'd like to formally introduce myself. My name is Adrian Abrams, a sophomore here and am really excited about taking your class."

"That's great to hear. I'm happy to have you Adrian."

"Thanks professor. After looking over the syllabus, I must express a couple of concerns however. For one, this is significantly more reading than I'm used to. Secondly, I've never written a paper longer than 8 pages yet I see a 12-15 page research paper here. Do you have any tips on how to go about both of these challenges for me?"

"Thank you for informing me of your concerns. Also, thank you for doing you due diligence and reading over the syllabus. In regards to the reading, I'm not sure if anyone has ever told you this, but you don't have to read every single word. Instead, college is about selective reading to the point where you can grab the big ideas and any related details. This does not require and extensive reading of the whole thing; especially if the assigned reading is 30 pages a night.

In regards to the research paper, the best advice I can offer is just by practicing. I purposely have assigned a 5 page essay and a 7 page essay as well to gauge my student's abilities as the required page count increases.

Actually, I'll tell you what. Make sure you stop in my office hours after each essay and we'll debrief your writing to ensure you're on the right track for the research paper at the end of the semester. In addition, as long as you give me 4 days in advance of the due date, I am willing to review the first two pages of each writing assignment to double check your thesis and see where your argument is heading."

"Wow, thanks so much for the great advice, professor! I'll be sure to follow up with you! I feel so much better about this course, especially given your willingness to ensure I do well."

My writing improved ten-fold this semester due to the guidance and close-watch of my professor. Not only that, but I received an "A" in the course after all was said and done. I made sure to follow up with my professor at the end to tie up any loose ends and express my gratitude for what they did for me.

"Hey professor! Do you have a moment?"

"Sure, come on in Adrian."

"I don't want to take too much of your time, but I wanted to express my sincerest gratitude for everything you did for me this semester. To be honest, I've never really had a professor invest in me to the extent that you did for this semester. My writing grew tremendously and I feel much more confident, in regards to writing intensive classes that I might have to take in the future; it's going to take a lot to intimidate me.

I truly am thankful for the genuine passion you have for your work and the investment that you show in us as students. I'll definitely be recommending your class to the underclassmen and whoever else may ask about it."

"I'm so glad to hear that, Adrian! As you mentioned, I take my craft very seriously and I'm glad that you found enjoyment and a lot of tangible takeaways from the course."

"For sure professor. Well, I hope you have a great break full of rest and relaxation! Be sure to stay in touch; I'd love to hear about new exciting ventures that you might have going on."

"Same to you, Adrian. By the way, let me know if you need me to write a letter of recommendation for you. You're a great student and it was an honor to witness your growth in my course over the semester first-hand."

By the end of the semester, I had my professor offering to write me a letter of recommendation whenever I needed it. Although many of you might chalk it up to luck, make no mistake about it:

Everything was intentional; this was by pure design.

* * *

A.T.T.E.N.DUE DILIGENCE.

ONE ON ONE IN OFFICE HOURS

In a study conducted by Mario Guerrero of the California Polytechnic University in Pomona and Alisa Beth Rod of the University of California, Santa Barbara found that office hour visits are positively correlated with academic performance.

The reason why is because for many students, one on one interaction with the professor can be the determining factor in their overall success in the class. College professors often have more discretion than high school students and if you are on the line between a B+ and an A-, then face-to-face, one-on-one interaction with your processor could be the difference. However, unlike high school, this time is far more scarce, especially if you are attending a large public institution.

One of the biggest outcomes that can stem from said one on one interaction is the professor giving you impactful insight as to what an assignment is asking of you, how you are currently performing in the class, steps you can take in order to better your performance, and things of that nature. Since your professor is the only one in a course that can break you, it also makes sense that your professor is the only one that can save you.

In addition, these one on one settings allow you the opportunity to advocate for yourself. If you have a hard time keeping up with the in-class material, whether that is due to external factors going on in your life or the material being increasingly difficult as you have never been exposed to it before, office hours can be just the setting you need in order to build a level of transparency with your professor that will be fruitful in the long run.

When establishing a sense of transparency, you are, in essence, becoming vulnerable with your professor. In general, being able to demonstrate vulnerability is a trait that many people admire. Therefore, your professor will appreciate this act because, if all else, it shows that you are serious about their class and are determined to get the most out of it.

Another hidden gem that can come from office hours is challenging grades that you received on assignments. In high school, you might have heard of the students that always sought after the best grade possible: "grade grubbers" if you will. No matter if you felt that was the right or wrong approach in high school, I would highly advise you to adopt that philosophy once you begin college.

Undoubtedly, the margin for error is that much higher in college, in comparison to high school. In high school, your teachers most likely gave out a good amount of homework, opportunities to retake tests, and in some cases even offered extra credit. In college, that narrative is few and far in between.

Your grades could be entirely dependent on 4 or 5 assignments for the entirety of a 16-week semester. In other words, you have to ensure that when deadlines are coming up, you have to rise to the occasion. However, I recognize that it is not always possible.

In situations where your actual grade falls shorter than what you projected your grade to be, there could be a variety of different explanations. For example, your output might not have been as good as you expected. Although you thought you were putting out quality A- work, your professor thought otherwise and gave you a B- instead.

If you ask anybody that knows me, they will tell you I never ascribe to the aforementioned rationale as I live by the philosophy, "challenge everything."

I think you should, too!

The other explanation can be simply explained: it was a case of misinterpretation. Perhaps the professor missed something pivotal in the assignment. Or they just flat out didn't give you credit where it was deserved. Instead of letting this strange occurrence go unnoticed, it would be to your benefit to have some due diligence and ensure you straighten out the misunderstanding.

Yeah, that makes a lot more sense.

I can speak to the optics of challenging grades in a class. Instead of just taking things for face value, you are seeking to gain a deeper understanding. The benefits of this are two-fold because 1) it shows the professor you are reflecting on past assignments and are serious about improving your performance and 2) you might end with a better grade on that assignment which will ultimately impact your overall grade in the class. Even if 1 happens without 2 or 2 happening without 1, it results in a win-win either way while the likelihood of neither 1 or 2 happening are slim.

Challenging grades is a short-term benefit to routinely attending office hours. Let's shift to long-term benefits.

When it comes to letters of recommendations, high school teacher letters can only be used for so long. As you traverse your undergraduate experience, you will find that many of the jobs, programs, and overall opportunities you are seeking will require letters of recommendations from faculty at your institution. In order for someone to be able to write a compelling letter for you, they must get to know you first. When you have a lecture hall filled with hundreds of students, what will separate you from them?

Office hours.

The fact of the matter is that most students are taking advantage of this hidden gem. Therefore, this is one of the most fruitful ways to distinguish yourself from your peers and, in essence, distinguish yourself from your competition.

Lastly, they can provide a wealth of knowledge that is not easily accessible to most people. Professors have a wealth of knowledge and can provide insight about a variety of different topics. Not only are they subject matter experts in their field of study, but they also were once in the same position that you are currently in. Therefore, they are great confidants when it comes to career advice or general trajectory.

How are you supposed to tap into this without actually using the dedicated time they set aside to get to know them?

HOW TO

Don't know how to navigate office hours? I've got you covered.

First things first: plan to attend office hours at least twice a month for each class. This is a good target to shoot for and will give you the necessary face-time with a professor to allow them to get to know you and address anything you see fit.

Below is advice for different scenarios for why you may be attending office hours.

- Attend office hours at the beginning of the semester. This is an opportunity to make a great first impression.
  - ◆ In addition, this is a great opportunity to lay out your expectations for the semester. Use the following framework: "I'm looking forward to learning about X, Y, and Z in this course. I'm determined to do well."
- Find out as much as you can about your professor beforehand.
  - ◆ Check their LinkedIn, discover research that they've gotten published, etc. People love to talk about themselves and this gives you enough ammo to deflect the conversation onto them.
- Sample questions
  - ◆ What path did you take to become a professor?
  - ◆ What do you find challenging and rewarding about being a professor?
  - ◆ Were you ever worried about __ when you were my age? Did you ever receive any advice on it?
  - ◆ What qualities or skills do you look for in a writer? Is this possible for your class?

WHEN TRYING TO ACADEMICALLY ADVOCATE FOR YOURSELF

- Do not come off as combative or emotional. Professors expect you to handle yourself as a rational adult and there is no quicker way for a professor to dismiss you than by letting your emotions guide the conversation.
- Have your argument clear, logical, and concise. Be prepared to

provide actual substantiation as professors are often unlikely to just take your word for it.

- Check in after every assignment. If you don't like your grade or think you should have done better, go in to your professor's office hours and talk about it. These are a great way to get points back that will add up come the end of the semester.
  - In addition, some professors offer revisions on assignments but don't feel the need to broadcast this to the class.
- Sample Questions/Phrases
  - *Beginning of the semester* I am very excited to take this course and hope to be performing at the highest level possible ultimately culminating in an A in the course. Although I am very eager about taking this course, I must admit, I am kind of nervous about the difficulty of the material. What do you think are some methods I should be incorporating in order to get the most out of the course and receive the best grade possible?
    - *As they give their response, jot the notes down in front of them. This is great for the optics.*
  - *End of semester* I see that my final grade is a B+ in the course. I was striving for an A- in the class and really thought I was understanding the material, as evidenced by my high level of participation and trying to do the little things right. Do you offer any opportunities for extra credit?
  - I'm extremely disappointed with my grade on this assignment. Where do you think I could have done better? Are you offering revisions for this assignment?

- The key here is to make sure you come in with specific questions related to class. NEVER say "I just don't get what's going on in class" as that is hard for a professor to react to. Instead, say "I don't understand ___ about the___ from the lecture/assignment on *insert day*."

- If you missed class, that's fine. Explain to them that you want to ensure you're taking all the necessary steps just in case you are behind. This is also great for the optics as it shows you are willing to follow up if you miss days. Most students don't care enough to do so.

- Don't be silent. Professors hate this during their office hours.

- If your question was answered within 3 minutes of talking with them, ensure you fully understand their feedback and don't have any other related questions. If not, don't feel forced to stay. Professors do value their time and they will appreciate you for this.

FINAL THOUGHTS

———

College is hard. I completely understand.

That's why I wanted to share my lessons learned with you.

If you apply these lessons in your collegiate setting, I promise you that you will receive a positive return on your investment.

As a quick reminder:

Attitude

Understand your the importance of your secondary schooling but don't let it be a factor that will either determine or inhibit your success. Come in with the mentality of an underdog and let sheer grit and resiliency be the guiding forces of how you will choose to navigate college. Nothing is given; everything must be earned.

Target

If you know your strengths, weaknesses, and passions before coming into college, it will help your collegiate learning curve and allow you to develop an effective strategy and plan of attack. If you don't know your strengths and interests, talk about it with those close to you to see what they have to say or utilize online resources. Research says identifying these aspects will lead to your academic success.

Why are you choosing college? What do you want to get out of your experience? Once these questions are answered, you will be able to reverse engineer your approach and craft the perfect strategy of attack for yourself.

Time

Don't take on too many extracurriculars. There is only so much time in the day and you want to ensure that whatever you are dedicating your time to is something you are passionate about. College is way too stressful to be stuck doing things you feel as though you're not interested in.

Time management will be imperative to your success. Not

only will this skill-set guide you to academic glory, it will also aid you in your navigation of post-graduate life. Once you have your time management skills in order, efficiency is the name of the game.

Efficiency

Once you've allocated enough time to accomplish everything in a given day, ensure you are operating at your most productive level. A trap that many students fall under is giving themselves enough time to complete something but wind up working at a slow pace or allowing external factors detract from their work.

iN-class participation

Participating in class is a sure fire method in improving your academic performance. Not only will you be able to engage with the class material and keep pace with the various topics discussed, you will also have a great platform to advocate on when trying to negotiate for a higher grade.

Due diligence

Office hours are another hidden gem in regards to academic excellency. Professors are people too and are subjective in their grading; leverage this to your advantage because it's hard to give a student you genuinely like a bad grade. Stemming from these one-on-one interactions include opportunities to obtain letters of recommendation, career advice, and extra help and supervision for various assignments.

Win your professors over. They hold their final grade in your hands. Get close to them; you have everything to gain.

The A.T.T.E.N.D. method has successfully allowed me, and underclassmen under my guidance, to hack college and, I must say, it feels damn good to be in the position that we're in now.

However, I'm not the type of person to want to keep all the wealth for myself. Take these lessons, apply them as you see fit, and win.

Let's Get It!

Made in the USA
San Bernardino, CA
20 July 2019